The Food of Love

A BOOK ABOUT COOKING

Guislaine Morland

With illustrations by Patrick Hughes

Chatto & Windus LONDON

Published in 1987 by Chatto & Windus Ltd
30 Bedford Square, London WC1B 3RP

British Library Cataloguing in Publication Data
Morland, Guislaine
    The food of love.
    1. Cookery, International
    I. Title
    641.5   TX725.A1

ISBN 0-7011-3230-2

Typeset by The Spartan Press Ltd, Lymington, Hants

Printed in Great Britain by
Redwood Burn Ltd, Trowbridge, Wiltshire

To
Tasha,
Georgia
and
Le Matou

Friends, which includes family, have eaten their way through this book, with enthusiasm and affection. Since I have changed the names of some, I thank them all as one. To my illustrator, I raise another and new glass. The table has outgrown its owner's imagination.

Contents

April

May

June

July

August

September

October

November

December

Prelude

One day, there was a house on a lake in New York State, a grandmother upstairs, a Bugatti in the garage; another day, dispersed and broke, we were staying at the Ritz in Barcelona because the concierge knew us from the days our flag flew high and big hotels are more patient than small hotels. It was the concierge you relied on for the 'sombra' side tickets to a bullfight, or the same quiet room as last time and for the bill to be postponed to mañana. The concierge sent us to the good local bars and restaurants, before the one-way stream of tourists got there. And we always ate well. Changing scenery and characters swept past as from the window of a train which started in North America, then South America, Spain, France, with a few short stops in England, Switzerland, Italy. Security was strung on a fragile chain of mirrors reflecting hope, luck and dreams which occasionally materialized into realities.

My nationality is a moot point. My father is French, born in Algiers, my mother is English, born in Sydney; neither was brought up in their country of birth. I was born in New York, but I learnt my multiplication tables in France and where you learn to count is where you keep your toys.

I examine these things, standing in the kitchen, stirring pots and memories. I am talking to the children, friends, answering the telephone, thinking of yesterday, today, or even tomorrow which is more difficult, while cooking dinner. I lay the table enjoying a decorative and sensual ritual. It is like painting a small picture, every day, over and over again, never quite the same. The narrow, precise shape of cutlery that frames the roundness of plates and the pepper pot that fits so comfortably into the palm of the hand; the texture of the red and white cloth napkins against the grain of the pine kitchen table I stained with olive oil; the bowl of fruit and the flowers in the deep blue pot brought back from Mexico a few years ago.

What follows is food provoked by memory and a routine. It is a personal view. I leave the experts to explain expertise.

Publisher's note and conversion tables

These recipes will feed 6–8 people, unless noted otherwise.

Both imperial and metric measurements are given. Use one or other set of measurements; do not mix the two.

It should be remembered that the American pint is 16 fl oz in comparison to the imperial pint, used in both Britain and Australia, which is 20 fl oz. The British standard tablespoon which has been used in the book holds 17.7 ml, the American 14.2 ml, and the Australian 20 ml. A teaspoon holds approximately 5 ml in all three countries.

Oven temperature chart

°C	°F	Gas mark	
110	225	¼	very slow
130	250	½	
140	275	1	slow
150	300	2	
170	325	3	
180	350	4	moderate
190	375	5	
200	400	6	moderately hot
220	425	7	hot
230	450	8	
240	475	9	very hot

Liquids

Imperial	Metric
2½ fl oz	75 ml
5 oz / ¼ pt	150 ml
10 oz / ½ pt	300 ml
20 oz / 1 pt	600 ml
1½ pt	900 ml
1¾ pt	1 litre
teaspoon	5 ml
dessertspoon	10 ml
tablespoon	15 ml

Solids

	Metric
1 oz	25 g
2 oz	50 g
4 oz	100 g
8 oz	225 g
12 oz	325 g
14 oz	400 g
16 oz / 1 lb	450 g

January

... The order was called through
to the kitchen as "Adam and Eve
on a raft"...

Giovanna and Lino come to stay; escape and return; Lino cooks

The day after Christmas, the children left with their father for a skiing trip in America and my oldest friend, Giovanna, came to stay. She arrived from Italy with her son, Massimo, and her new man, Lino. At midnight on December 31st, we observed the Italian custom of eating Parmesan, one piece each, the size of a Greek olive, for luck and prosperity. We washed it down with champagne, wishing for the best of both. Lentils bring similar gifts and we had those with a pheasant that had cooked with apples and lardons and cream. We discussed all our plans. Miles and I had separated six months ago, soon the house would be on the market and I was returning to the work I had started and stopped fifteen years before. Lino would be staying in London until a certain political scandal died down. I would help him to find a flat. Giovanna would fly over most week-ends to see him, incognito, as I would be the next day when I left on a voyage of impulse and folly. Giovanna and Lino would cover my tracks should anyone call, as I would theirs, in future. I arrived early, and, not having eaten on the plane, found myself being treated to two poached eggs on toast in a diner. The order was called through to the kitchen as 'Adam and Eve on a raft'.

I returned to London, muddled with jet-lag, three days later, on the early morning flight. There was Lino, frying eggs for his breakfast. Sunny side up, I thought, still on another wave length. I slept for most of that day and in the evening Lino and Giovanna prepared a risotto. Their way turned out to be quicker than my own and, I reluctantly admitted, just a little better. It was kept at a highish bubble and at the end, while arguing with Giovanna about her mannish taste in clothes, Lino added a small handful of grated Parmesan and melted it into the rice with a tablespoon of butter. When you are tired, rice is comforting and unargumentative. Giovanna, between sips of wine and mouthfuls of risotto alle tartuffi di Lino, warned me against Transatlantic Affairs and brought me back down to earth. Lino chided her for being harsh and humourless. I have known Giovanna since the age of eight and her affection is like that of a sister, just older enough to be wiser and even stern. Her advice and perspective were needed.

We ended the meal with a panettone in a sabayon sauce.

Faisan pour Giovanna et Lino

Melt 4–5oz / 100–125g smoked BACON or PANCETTA, diced, in a cast iron pot and cook until almost crisp. Remove with a slotted spoon, set aside. Brown the PHEASANT on all sides in the bacon fat, adding a little BUTTER or PEANUT OIL if necessary. Discard any burnt fat; scatter the cooked pieces of bacon or pancetta around the bird, with a few chopped SHALLOTS and one Granny Smith APPLE, peeled and cut into small pieces. Pour in half a bottle of dry-ish WHITE WINE, scraping up the solids off the bottom of the pan. Add a little SALT and PEPPER. Cover and simmer 40 minutes to one hour.

The lid of my cast iron pot has a rim on the underside which makes the evaporation dribble back down the pot; if this is not the case, check the level of cooking liquid and, if necessary, add a little wine. Remove the pheasant to a serving platter and keep warm in a barely heated oven. Turn up the heat under the cast iron pot, pour in a glass of MADEIRA and reduce the sauce by half. Turn down to a gentle simmer; add double CREAM to taste, but the sauce should not look pale. The gamy taste of the pheasant is drawn into the sauce and makes it taste slightly smoky — a refreshing change after a couple of months of roast game. Pour the sauce over the pheasant and sprinkle with freshly chopped parsley.

Or, soak a handful of dried MORELS or CEPS in hot water for 10–15 minutes. Brown the pheasant as above, add shallots and a tablespoon of FENNEL SEEDS. Dilute TOMATO PURÉE and Dijon MUSTARD – about a tablespoon of each to 1 cup of liquid – with RED WINE and the liquor from the mushrooms. Pour this in, with the morels or ceps. Cook in red wine as above. Serve either with LENTILS or STRING BEANS with turnipped PEARS (see pp 5 and 6).

Leftover pheasant: separate thighs and drumsticks. Cook a few SAUSAGES, perhaps venison, and a few pieces of BACON.

Scrape the pan with a glass of RED WINE and STOCK, simmer
10 minutes. Add pheasant pieces and stir with the sausages until
warmed up. Thicken the sauce if necessary, with a little
MUSTARD then a dash of TABASCO and WORCESTERSHIRE
SAUCE.

Or, turn the lentils into a robust soup, adding pieces of the
pheasant at the end.

Lentilles Porte-Bonheur

I use French LENTILS. They are smaller, firmer and less pasty
than ones usually sold in London. Not having been able to find
them in England, I have a network of friends who return from
France with a packet or three in their suitcase. They are found
easily in France as lentilles vertes. Some brand names: Aigle,
Dupuy, Legumor.

After checking the lentils for grit and pebbles, cover with
CHICKEN STOCK or when in season, that of game. Use RED
WINE if you don't have stock, but not water. For 1lb / 450g
lentils, add 3 broken BAY LEAVES, 4 or 5 chopped cloves of
GARLIC, 3 generous pinches each of ALLSPICE and CHINESE
FIVE SPICES. Put in a branch of CELERY, 1 CARROT, chopped
and 1 or 2 small ONIONS spiked with CLOVES. Bring very
slowly to a simmer; it should take at least half an hour to 45
minutes to reach that point. Simmer, covered, for about 40
minutes. Time and absorption vary according to type and age of
lentils. Check occasionally that all is well and that they are not
ready before you expect them to be. They should be almost firm,
but giving, like rice. When they reach the al dente stage, I turn off
the heat and let them sit. This way they do not overcook.

If any liquid remains, drain but reserve the liquid for soup or
even as a base for a gravy when roasting. Check the seasoning,
add freshly ground PEPPER and SALT to your taste, then
BUTTER.

For a salad: omit the vegetables during the cooking. When cool,
add freshly chopped GARLIC, at least a dozen chopped SPRING
ONIONS and a generous quantity of fresh PARSLEY and MINT,
chopped. By generous I mean at least 2 teacupfuls of each; this

makes all the difference. Dress with a strong OLIVE OIL and a good VINEGAR such as sherry or cider. Mix with your hands so as not to bruise the lentils. They will continue to absorb. Check later that they don't need more dressing. Serve as is or with crumbled GOAT CHEESE or FETA, ANCHOVIES and black Niçoise OLIVES. If you refrigerate the lentils, remove at least 2 hours before eating as the oil solidifies and the dressing loses its taste.

Any leftover lentils make a delicious strong *soup*. Add RED WINE, a little water or STOCK, a few chopped TOMATOES. Simmer for at least an hour, this time letting the lentils overcook and gently turn into a purée.

Or, bake leftover lentils in a hot oven for 15 to 20 minutes with a few pieces of SMOKED BACON, SAUSAGES or leftover GOOSE SKIN, sprinkled generously with grated GRUYÈRE and PAR-MESAN.

String Beans with Turnipped Pears

This is a derivation of a recipe from Moira Hodgson in the *New York Times*, taken from Alexander Dumas' account of the Court of Wurtemberg kitchen. I use Bosc pears, rather than Bartlett as she suggested, being firmer.

Prepare and blanch fine FRENCH STRING BEANS. Drain. Peel 1 PEAR per person. Slice in half and across once more into a more turnip-like shape. Blanch for 3–4 minutes in boiling water, drain. Cook the pears in a frying pan with a little BACON and its fat, a dash of white SUGAR, 1 tablespoon of CIDER VINEGAR, NUTMEG, SALT and PEPPER. Let the pears brown a little as the sauce caramelises. Add the string beans and toss until they are warmed, adding a little BUTTER if necessary.

Sauce Sabayonnée

Beat 6 EGG YOLKS, gradually adding 5–6 tablespoons of GRANULATED SUGAR, then a generous 4oz / 100g of SAUTERNES or dark RUM or even MADEIRA or MARSALA. Turn the mixture into the top of a double boiler and whisk energetically over simmering water until it foams and thickens.

This should only take about 5 minutes or less. Test with your finger. Remove from heat when it feels bearably hot to the touch.

Pour into a china bowl standing in iced water. Continue whisking until cool and even thicker.

To taste, add 4 or 5 tablespoons of DOUBLE CREAM; or CRÈME FRAÎCHE if you can find it; if not, use strained Greek YOGHURT mixed with double cream, preferably Jersey.

Risotto di Lino

The most prized Italian white TRUFFLE is found around chestnut trees. Should you have one, trap it in a jar with about 12oz / 300g ARBORIO RICE, depending on your appetite. I allow 3oz /75g of rice per person. Let the rice absorb the truffle's scent for 24 hours, which it will do powerfully. You can do the same to a bowl of EGGS, well covered. The next day, scramble them. The strength of taste is surprising.

Have ready, and gently simmering, a good CHICKEN STOCK, about 1¾ pts / 1 litre. Don't bother to make risotto without stock. Quantity of stock varies according to the rice you use. This should be enough for 12oz / 300g of rice, to serve four people.

In a deep cast iron or copper casserole melt a finely chopped ONION in BUTTER and OLIVE OIL until it begins to colour. Add the rice when the butter sizzles and the onion has softened. Stir for a minute or two until the rice absorbs the butter and turns opaque. Pour in a small glass of WHITE WINE, stir for a few seconds, add stock to just cover the rice. Maintain a steady bubble, between a simmer and boil. Continue stirring gently with a wooden spoon. Add stock as the level drops below that of the rice. Don't let the rice stick to the pan. Keep adding stock and stirring. After 20 minutes, reduce the amount of stock as the risotto should be ready in 5 or 10 minutes at the most. Taste. The rice should be creamy, each grain separate, barely coated with the syrupy, reduced stock, giving on the outside, al dente within; there should be a barely visible line of liquid at the edges of the pan.

Add a tablespoon of freshly grated PARMESAN (never from a box) and stir in with a knob of BUTTER.

I serve this risotto sprinkled with fresh SAGE and PARSLEY,

to cut the richness. The taste of truffle will be strong but, if you are greedy, grate a little on to the rice using a grater that produces thin slivers the size of small leaves. In this case, omit the sage.

Of course, the risotto is just as good, in a different way, without the truffle. Add a few pieces of CHICKEN, just 2 or 3 tablespoons of meat diced, or 3 or 4 CHICKEN LIVERS, previously fried. Italians usually serve the risotto quite wet.

The next day there was a little risotto left over. Lino made little round *pancakes* with it and fried them with an EGG on the side. Delicious.

The telephone rings too often; make soup instead of answering; a French grandmother; les fourmis

The children returned the second week, just in time for school, tanned by the sun in Taos Ski Valley. Tasha, then twelve, presented me with a tin of Sante Fé chocolate chip cookies, and my nine year old Georgia explained that they were very chewy. On the lid of the tin was a picture of a Wild West train. Giovanna and Massimo returned to Italy and Lino found a small house in South Kensington. We spoke to each other most days. Giovanna's presence had accelerated our knowledge of each other, increasing a familiarity that would have otherwise taken years, if ever, to reach. Lino watched and laughed as I zigzagged like a bumper car into lawyers, butchers, accountants, bakers: 'Only half of you is pazza [mad], the other half is reliable – so what, accept it', he said, as I tried to keep life in order although my thoughts and instincts were chaos.

The weather in London was as cold as could be expected. Most evenings, we had soup. Tasha's favourite is carrot and Georgia's is tomato. Or is it the other way around. I often confuse their preferences, but at least one is pleased, as is the other next time. The phone rang incessantly that month. The sound of its ring at certain times of day frightened me and making soups was a restful and simple escape. I used to look forward to my French grandmother's potages, as I did to her monthly reading of my palm and cards. Both were as soothing as a gentle massage, as she touched my hands following the lines of life and luck. I lived with her in New York for a few years before and after turning twenty. She used to rise early to make herself un grand café au lait, then return to bed in her apartment overlooking the East River and a flashing Pepsi Cola sign. She read *France-Amérique* and the *New*

York Herald Tribune – pronounced Le Eral – through pink and slightly smudged glasses. She sipped her coffee noisily and her toes waved slightly, forming an éventail, as the French say. The small, restless movements of hands and feet were really to alleviate what she called les fourmis dans mes jambes – a problem of circulation.

Her name was Marguerite. To me and to her other seven grand-children, she was Ninin – a variation of Nana. Her forehead was high and wide, the size of her ears intrigued me and she had what she called appreciatively le nez des Bourbons. She was a little plump, in a neat way. She moved with precise short steps in all directions, looking vague and cheerful, half-humming, half-whistling something like 'Marl-borough s'en va-t-en Guerre' or 'Les Plaisirs d'Amour'. She topped up her alimony by drawing up astrological charts for the United Nations diplomatic community, which embarrassed us, but her following was loyal and as widespread as her reputation. I used to sit on her bed, late at night, sucking the honey and lemon sweets from the porcelain box at her bedside. I listened to stories of heat and perfume from North Africa – Rabat, Mostaganem. Fruit orchards and white dresses; her favourite cousin; her intended, who was a spahi to whom she sent secret messages via her Arab servant's shopping basket. The last taste on the palate being the one that lingers, I could only just perceive the ghost of the young woman speaking from within the shell of my grandmother today. 'Ninin Fourmis' who used to play tennis in a long dress. I remember so little now, other than a faint impression of scent, like that of a woman walking past in the street. Yet I find myself, at forty, repeating some of her gestures. Through smudged but large tortoise-shell glasses, I read the papers in bed, sipping my café au lait, but doucement, à l'anglaise. My toes wave, as do those of my elder daughter Tasha, I noticed the other day. And Georgia has pointed out that she too waves her feet. The only difference, she says, is that 'my toes haven't grown enough yet'. By nine o'clock, like Ninin, I am dressed and before getting to work, make myself un toast. If we are to have un potage le soir, I make it shortly afterwards. It rests during the day and tastes even better in the evening.

Potage de Broccoli et Cresson

The colour of this soup somehow makes you feel well just to look at it, let alone after eating it. Because the vegetables are only just cooked, the taste is fresh and green. For four people, soften 2 chopped ONIONS and 2 chopped SHALLOTS in BUTTER. Add

2 small POTATOES, peeled and cubed. Cover with 2½ pints / 1.25 l of CHICKEN STOCK and simmer for 5 minutes. Add the trimmed stalks of a dozen BROCCOLI branches, chopped. Simmer another 5 minutes. Add the broccoli flower heads. Simmer 3 minutes more. Then 2 bunches of WATERCRESS, including most of the stalks. Cover for 1 minute. Remove the vegetables with a slotted spoon and reduce to a purée in the blender or Magimix or mouli. Return to the broth. If too thick, dilute to your taste with a little milk. Add a generous amount of chopped, fresh PARSLEY and a little CREAM.

If using the blender, stop before the mixture becomes finely blended, as this can make the texture a little gluey.

Potage de Laitue et Poulet

The day after roasting a CHICKEN, place the carcass, wings and thighs, if left over, and any remaining gravy, into a stockpot. Cover with water, add half a bottle of WHITE WINE. Bring to a boil; skim the froth and foam that will rise at simmering point. Add 5 or 6 GARLIC cloves, 1 ONION, a stalk of CELERY and 1 CARROT, all chopped, a couple of BOUQUETS GARNIS, a dash of TABASCO and WORCESTERSHIRE SAUCE. Simmer at a bare quiver, for six or seven hours, or even better, overnight, covered tightly with foil and lid, sitting on an asbestos pad.

Strain the stock through a fine sieve into a clean saucepan. Add 4 large POTATOES, peeled and cubed, a good pinch of SAFFRON, 4 or 5 fresh cloves of GARLIC, whole. Simmer for an hour or until the potatoes start to disintegrate. Check for seasoning, add any leftover pieces of CHICKEN and 2 handfuls of shredded LETTUCE (not crisp lettuce, such as Iceberg or Cos). Serve just as the lettuce starts to wilt, with a cupful of chopped PARSLEY. At table, swirl a knob of BUTTER in your bowl or even a spoonful of leftover AÏOLI or ROUILLE. When you find a whole clove of garlic, crush it with your spoon. It will be sweet and soft.

This will serve 4 people.

Potage de Carottes

Soften 2 chopped ONIONS in BUTTER; add a dozen medium CARROTS, chopped finely. Cook, stirring, for a few minutes, until the carrots start to stick and caramelise just a little. Add a little more BUTTER, if necessary. Cover with 2½ pints / 1.25l of CHICKEN STOCK, add a handful of ARBORIO RICE. Simmer until the rice is done. Remove the vegetables, using a slotted spoon, and reduce to a purée in a mouli or in a Magimix. Don't use a blender. Return to the broth. Add a little MILK to achieve your desired consistency, or a little single CREAM, a generous quantity of chopped PARSLEY, a few SAGE leaves, chopped, SALT and freshly ground PEPPER. Any leftover smoked HAM is a delicious addition, ground quite finely. This serves 4 people.

Potage de Tomates et Poivron Rouge

The RED PEPPER in this soup is important. Its taste is barely noticeable, but it gives the tomato soup a richer taste and subtle scent, somehow fresh. For once, water is preferable to stock.

Soften 2 ONIONS in BUTTER and PEANUT OIL, with 1 finely chopped CARROT and 1 large RED PEPPER, seeded and chopped. Add a 14oz / 400g tin of Italian PLUM TOMATOES, 1½ pints / 900ml of water, a strip of ORANGE PEEL, a little pinch of SAFFRON (unless you particularly dislike its definite taste), a good pinch of GROUND FENNEL, a handful of ARBORIO RICE, a dash of SALT, an even smaller dash of SUGAR. Simmer until the rice is done. Make a purée of the solids in the blender and return to broth. Add a little single CREAM and freshly chopped PARSLEY. Check the seasoning.

This quantity serves 4.

Potage de Moules

This is more than a potage, and fairly elegant as a starter, both in taste and appearance.

Prepare a STOCK made with LOBSTER SHELLS, CRAB SHELLS, SHRIMP HEADS AND SHELLS – when you buy the MUSSELS, your fishmonger, with a little coaxing, should provide you with your stock needs. See page 51. Allow 2½ pints / 1.25l of this stock for 4 people.

Sweat 1 medium ONION, chopped, in OLIVE OIL, until soft,

with 1 heaped tablespoon of FENNEL SEEDS. Add 2 POTATOES, peeled and roughly diced; 1 bulb of FENNEL, chopped. Stir for a few minutes with the onion and cover with the stock. Simmer gently until the vegetables are soft. Make a purée of the vegetables in a blender with a ladle of liquid. Return to the pot, add 1 teaspoon of CHINESE FIVE SPICES or a few drops of PERNOD – almost a shot-size glass.

Steam about 3 handfuls of fresh mussels, in their shells, with a small glass of WHITE WINE. As soon as they open, remove from heat, add their liquor to the soup. Take the mussels out of their shells (although sometimes I put them in the soup; it looks nice and the mussels are easy enough to pry loose with a spoon), putting them into the soup just as you are warming it up again to serve. Heat gently, adding a little single CREAM, a knob of BUTTER and freshly ground PEPPER and SALT to taste.

More about Ninin; Paris

Ninin was a natural and distracted cook. Many were the times that a strange smell led me to a shelf or cupboard where I would find her 'lost' sauce, or a forgotten hen from her butcher, Monsieur Albert, on the corner of First Avenue and 51st Street. She entertained often; her dinners and parties were a slightly dishevelled success. Her guests were a mixture of two, if not three, generations. It seemed eccentric to me at the time but I think now, with the distance of age, that it is perhaps Gallic. Nationalities and background were as mixed as the china and cutlery, sets having been broken up by various children, grandchildren, life and war. She was unsentimental, strong, fiercely loyal. And habits die hard – her couscous was the real thing.

New York was home; she spent thirty odd years there with a French accent that increased each year. Then ten years ago, in May, she left New York in an uncharacteristic hurry. First, she summoned me to her apartment, to give me a list of belongings with instructions as to whom they should be distributed, adding that I was to be her executrix. She was energetic and pert. It seemed unnecessary. I wasn't pleased with the task. She laughed and agreed the position might not be enviable. She then called my father, her eldest child, who was living in Paris. She told him she was arriving. She wanted to see the rest of the family. Not an easy task with such little warning, but my father, whose motto seems to be never complain, never explain, arranged the gathering. He called other cities in other countries. His two sisters came the next day, with most of their children. The table was laid for ten, the food prepared, the wine opened. After lunch, most dispersed. Miguel, her second grand-child, remained. They played canasta. She had a stroke and was taken to hospital unconscious. She died without regaining consciousness a few hours later. Ninin's affection had always been unconditional, as was her farewell.

Le Couscous de Ninin

What follows is Ninin's method, passed on to my father, passed on to me. Each time, like a snowball gathering speed and size as it rolls, the recipe takes on a little more as it passes through a different hand. Couscous recipes are elusive, as those for a cassoulet or bouillabaisse, the good reason being that these meals are stories told to one family in one region, from another family in another region. There are no firm and fast rules, except for the handling of the grain and even that varies a little.

Only make a couscous when you are relaxed, pleased with the rhythm of life and have two or three days to devote to its making. What follows will feed 8 people.

The Harissa Prepare one, even two days in advance. For the harissa, as my father says, you employ the 'partridge method': cook one partridge, throw away, cook a partridge, referring to the classic French recipe for perdrix aux choux.

Prepare a mirepoix of vegetables such as 2 CARROTS, 2 branches of CELERY, 2 large ONIONS, 2 LEEKS, perhaps a PARSNIP. Simmer with a little CHICKEN STOCK and a 14oz / 400g tin of Italian PLUM TOMATOES for half an hour. Sieve into a bowl, pushing through a little of the mirepoix itself. Throw away the rest. Add to the liquid a cup of freshly chopped, seeded and peeled TOMATOES, 2 finely chopped and seeded RED PEPPERS, 1 or 2 hot CHILLI PEPPERS, chopped, 4 cloves of GARLIC finely chopped, 2 teaspoons of CUMIN SEEDS or CARAWAY SEEDS depending on your inclination that day, a few strands of SAFFRON, 3 pinches of CINNAMON. The sauce should be fiery hot, but not so much that you can't taste it. Its thickness is that of single cream. Add 2 handfuls of CHICKPEAS, previously soaked and cooked al dente in a strong LAMB or CHICKEN STOCK. Simmer for an hour and set aside.

The Ratatouille   Make this as you like it, enough for 6 people even though this whole recipe is for eight. There is so much on one's plate at the end, that a small helping of each is enough. We tend to make a ratatouille that is quite thick, cooking it to the point where the vegetables are almost indistinguishable and slightly caramelised but wet. See page 54.

La Marmelade d'Oignons   Stew 12 large ONIONS, sliced (not chopped), very slowly, in OLIVE OIL, a little BUTTER, SALT and PEPPER, CUMIN SEEDS, CINNAMON, tiny pieces of FRESH GINGER, following the method described in the recipe for a pissaladière. See page 43. At the end, add a pinch of SUGAR and a few RAISINS. Set aside.

The Grain   On the morning of your dinner, prepare the SEMO-LINA grain, having found, with difficulty, the large grain, or failing that, the medium one. Allow 3oz / 75g per person at least. It has usually been pre-cooked, but only in the way that rice has been treated. Put the grain into a large bowl, sprinkle with lukewarm water, a little OLIVE OIL and SALT. Rub the grain between the palms of your hands, distributing the water, oil and salt evenly and insistently, as it doesn't absorb willingly. Do this for 5 or 10 minutes, adding a little more water, only a few more drops of oil, less and less as you go along. It is like playing with sand. Keep rolling the grain with your hands. It should at first feel a little sticky, slowly less and less so, finally, not at all. Now spread out several tea towels on the counters or on the kitchen table. Spread the grain on the towels and leave to dry for most of the day. To make sure each grain is separate, we end up with couscous everywhere, on all tables, all counters. The house seems full of it.

And now the family divides. My father dislikes the poulet bouilli des Français. The French don't know un vrai couscous, he says, implying two things: that to know couscous you must be a Pied Noir and that the real Frenchman *is* a Pied Noir, which takes us back to ce traître, de Gaulle as Ninin called him, and the conversation takes fire like the harissa . . . Here is my father's method.

Use a boned or 'butterflied' LEG OF LAMB. Cut into pieces and brown in the frying pan with OLIVE OIL. Place in a baking dish with fresh olive oil, and rub with broken BAY LEAVES, CUMIN powder and fresh THYME. Let it rest for a few hours, or overnight if you decide to do this ahead of time, as with the harissa.

Prepare the vegetables for the bouillon: an hour before dinner, fill the bottom of the couscoussière (a large steaming pot) with chopped CABBAGE leaves, CARROTS, CELERY, TURNIPS, ONIONS, GARLIC and SEASONING. Cover with water or STOCK. Line the top part of the steamer, usually a fine sieve, with one or two tea towels and put in the dried COUSCOUS grain. Cover, wrap the pan with another tea towel around its waist, where bottom meets top. Steam the grain for an hour and bake the lamb in the oven at the same time, or just a little earlier, and keep warm and pink. Remove the grain when it is still slightly al dente to a large serving bowl. Fluff it up with your hands or a couple of forks, rubbing out any balls that may have formed. Put in lots of BUTTER and a little OLIVE OIL. Distribute evenly.

To serve, start with a helping of the couscous grain, moisten with a ladleful of the bouillon, then a helping of the ratatouille, the marmalade of onions, then the lamb and, finally, a spoonful, or two if you are stoic, of the harissa.

Or, to contradict my father, half way through the cooking of the grain add to the bouillon pieces of chicken and any other meats. Serve these, and the vegetables from the broth with the ladleful of bouillon on the couscous grain.

Remembering snows of Beaver Dam; eating too much

Went for a cold walk in the country, with Lino and Miles. As they talked, getting on well, I mentally drifted between them, arm in arm with each: a husband in limbo on the left, a large buffer on the right. The children ran ahead, around, behind, like small winds. Another year would pass before the divorce went through, but I didn't know this and wondered how long it would be.

January in 'Beaver Dam' – the house in New York State we left three years ago – was a good month to think of. The heavy snows outside the door kept noise at bay and social life down to essentials. Only close friends attempted the long and treacherous driveway to the house. We went for long walks, followed by our marmalade cat who invariably howled by the tree he had once got stuck in. On other days of deep snow, Miles would put on his cross-country skis by the front door, disappear silently and quickly. The corridors of the house were cold but they led to a fire in the sitting room which I laid and lit by noon. On the way to the kitchen, I would rub my hands over it, then turn my back and warm the rest, muttering to myself about le froid des Amériques. We ate for warmth and we ate too well, it now seems. Beans baked for two days, slowly, with herbs and brown sugar and Bourbon; flageolets spiking the digestion with an arrabbiata sauce; leeks melted in butter and cream, a favourite of Miles', usually given precedence as a starter; butternut squash baked with bacon, ginger and brown sugar, forming a pool in its well of good things melted; Miles' open omelette which came from a recipe of Judith Olney but which gathered, each time, a little more: peas, croûtons, tomatoes, pancetta. And then sausages.

An Open Omelette

A perfect omelette made with two perfect eggs is a perfect meal in itself – a little creamy and runny in the middle, sprinkled with a few fresh herbs and chives. I have never mastered the technique, my wrist doesn't 'flick' and invariably the trip from pan to plate is a disaster. So either Miles cooked it or I made an open omelette, a satisfying and greedy way of using up the leftovers of a good lunch or dinner.

The following is a rough guide, for four people.

Prepare a basic mixture of 1 ONION, chopped, 1 GARLIC clove, finely chopped. Cook both in a little OIL and BUTTER until soft and changing colour. Fry 2 medium POTATOES, peeled and cubed, in the same pan until browned, almost crisp. Combine all these ingredients in a bowl. To them add what you may have left over, such as a generous cupful of RATATOUILLE, crumbled SAUSAGES, some PEAS, COURGETTES, ASPARA-GUS or WATERCRESS. Mix well but lightly.

Beat 10 EGGS, season them with HERBS and freshly ground
PEPPER (not salt, as this toughens the eggs). Pour the eggs into
the mixture and combine gently. Preheat the grill.

Heat a large cast iron pan, or the perfect omelette pan if you
have it, about 8–10in / 20–25cm in diameter with enough
BUTTER to film the bottom of the pan. As the butter sizzles and
starts to brown, pour in the egg mixture. Distribute evenly with a
fork, scratching at the bottom of the pan. Sprinkle a handful of
grated COMTÉ cheese or PARMESAN, add 2 or 3 tablespoons of
single CREAM, without mixing. This should not have taken more
than 1½ minutes, the omelette should still be runny in the centre.
Put the pan under the grill for another minute or two, until the
omelette sets, only just, and the edges brown. Sprinkle with fresh
PARSLEY and CHIVES. Serve immediately.

There will be a light coating of cream and melted cheese over
the filling, adding to the moistness of the just-cooked omelette.
Sometimes, if particularly greedy and hungry on a cold day, I will
scatter on a few croûtons, for a crunchy contrast.

Leeks melted in Cream

Allow 2 perfect LEEKS per person, avoiding the giant-sized
vegetable sold with such pride. Clean and trim, leaving
1in / 2cm, at least, of green. Slice once lengthwise. Cook gently in
warmed BUTTER in a frying pan for 5 minutes. Turn the leeks
over carefully, add single CREAM to not quite cover them.
Simmer 5 minutes more with a pinch of SALT, freshly ground
PEPPER and freshly grated NUTMEG.

The cream takes on a hint of the leeks' oniony taste. We used to
have these leeks on fried BREAD and a slice of Vermont
SMOKED HAM. Little more than a salad and fruit afterwards is
sufficient.

Butternut Squash

The flesh of these squash is the same colour as that of the
pumpkin but it is more dense, with a hint of chestnut in its
flavour. A small pumpkin is almost as good. These squash have
patches of yellow against the dark green. Choose the ones with
the bigger yellow patches. Cut each SQUASH in half, remove the

seeds. In each small well, place a knob of BUTTER, a slice of BACON cut in 4 pieces, 1 tablespoon of dark brown SUGAR, a pinch of SALT, freshly and coarsely ground PEPPER, 1/2 teaspoon of ground GINGER. Bake in a medium hot oven for 45–60 minutes.

So Many Carrots

Slice the best CARROTS you can find into very thin rounds. Sweat in BUTTER, in a heavy pan, stirring, until cooked. Add a pinch of SALT and freshly ground PEPPER, a little single CREAM, 1 small ONION cut into airmail paper-thin slices, PARSLEY. Serve immediately, before the onion cooks. The slight crunch of raw onion, barely noticeable, is mysterious and delicious. 2 or 3 tablespoons of grated RADISH or CAULI-FLOWER, raw, are another nice teaser.

Or, sweat in butter as above with slivers of fresh GINGER and a dash of BROWN SUGAR. As they cook and caramelise, add the cream.

Or, grate at least 2 carrots per person. Heat a cast iron frying pan with a generous quantity of butter. Put in the carrots at medium heat, pack them down, sprinkle with salt and freshly ground pepper. Leave alone for 10 to 15 minutes, or until a peek underneath shows that the carrots are blackening. Turn over, like a pancake, and cook in the same way on the other side. Don't be afraid to let the carrots blacken; the taste is interesting and good.

Beaver Dam Baked Beans

There is something reassuring about beans cooking slowly in winter, the smell filling the kitchen, teasing the appetite.

Soak 1lb / 450g of KIDNEY BEANS overnight. Drain and rinse. Bring to a boil in a saucepan with WHITE WINE and a rich STOCK to cover the beans; add any leftover GRAVIES. Remove the beans with a slotted spoon to a deep enamelled cast-iron casserole or earthenware pot with tight-fitting lid. Stir in 2 tablespoons dark BROWN SUGAR, 2 tablespoons MAPLE SYRUP, 5–6 fl oz / 140–170ml of MOLASSES, 1 teaspoon of

GROUND GINGER, 1 tablespoon TOMATO PURÉE, 1 table-spoon of hot Dijon MUSTARD, 1 large ONION, finely chopped, 4 cloves of GARLIC, finely chopped. Dice 8oz / 225g of SALT PORK, PANCETTA or SMOKED BACON – whichever is the best you can find. Add this to the beans, with a SMOKED HAM HOCK. Return enough of the cooking liquid to not quite cover the beans. Bake, tightly covered, for 7 or 8 hours or overnight in a low oven. Check occasionally that the beans are bathed in enough liquid. Leave the beans to rest for a day. Remove the ham hock.

Reheat on the third day in a medium hot oven for about half an hour, uncovered. Sprinkle on a few fresh BREADCRUMBS and baste so that a crust forms. Sprinkle with fresh PARSLEY and any fresh HERBS you may still have.

Cannellini Arrabiata

Soak 1lb / 450g of FLAGEOLETS or CANNELLINI in cold water for a morning or overnight. Drain and rinse. Put into a large saucepan, cover with RED WINE and a good rich STOCK and any leftover GRAVIES. Bring as slowly as possible to the boil – this should take at least 30 minutes. Maintain the boil for 10 minutes (this is to make sure toxins are destroyed), then lower to a simmer. Add a piece of PORK RIND or lean pieces of SMOKED BACON, and a PIG'S TROTTER; ½ teaspoon of ALLSPICE, ½ teaspoon of CHINESE FIVE SPICES, a broken BAY LEAF, 3 or 4 cloves of chopped GARLIC, 1 medium ONION, chopped. Simmer gently, covered, for 1 hour – perhaps a little less, a little more, depending on the age and variety of beans used, and the firmness you prefer.

Remove the various meats. Check the level of the liquid. The beans should be moist, but not swimming. Taste for seasoning, add SALT and freshly ground PEPPER to your taste. Cut into bite sizes any meats you have left over, such as LAMB or SMOKED HAM, PANCETTA, good SAUSAGES, freshly made FRANK-FURTERS (not any other kind), pieces of PHEASANT or VENISON. Lay the beans and meats in a gratin dish, surround with a thick ribbon of ARRABBIATA SAUCE, (see page 20), put in a medium hot oven and bake until the sauce begins to caramelise. Serve with freshly grated PARMESAN or PECORINO, chopped PARSLEY and SAGE.

Arrabbiata Sauce

There are endless versions of this sauce. This is my own which I use often – with cannellini beans; a mould of cooked ground lamb with spices, rosewater, raisins (see page 169); on spaghetti, or with a firm fish such as haddock or cod.

Heat 3 tablespoons of OLIVE OIL with 3 tablespoons of BUTTER in an enamelled cast-iron frying pan. Add 1 large ONION, finely chopped and 6 cloves of GARLIC, finely chopped. Cook until soft and changing colour, stirring to prevent any burning. Add 4 tablespoons each of CELERY, CARROT and FENNEL, all finely chopped. Cook gently, stirring, for a good 5 minutes. Add a small glass of MILK; stir until the milk evaporates and the vegetables start to stick and brown.

Sprinkle with a pinch of SALT and freshly ground NUTMEG. Add 1 (or 2 if you like heat) small, hot CHILLI PEPPER, seeded and chopped finely, a 14oz / 400g tin of Italian PLUM TOMATOES and a glass of WHITE WINE. Break up the tomatoes, cook as gently and slowly as possible for 3–4 hours. During the last half hour, add a BOUQUET GARNI. Check the seasoning. A pinch of INSTANT COFFEE and ALLSPICE will deepen the taste and correct any acidity.

This sauce gets better every day and freezes well.

Sausages in tears; getting greedier; multiplying; moving

The first two years of our decade in the Westchester countryside were spent in an old clapboard house overlooking Pea Pond through an alley of dogwood trees that would bloom on alternate years. The pond was small; it took ten minutes to row along its perimeter, or twenty if we lingered by the little island in the middle to note the activity of Canadian geese, nesting, or catch a glimpse of a snapping turtle noting the same interesting event. By our second November at Pea Pond House I was eight months pregnant feeling, this second time, too big and clumsy. Miles came home one Saturday morning with a meat grinder and a stuffing machine for sausages. That evening, we started. The ground meats of lamb and beef, or was it pork and veal, had been mixed with herbs, spices and saltpetre, only one slice of white bread soaked in a reduction of red wine and stock ('not very English', said Miles). We had ground the meats through the coarse blade first, then a second time through the finer blade. The intestinal skins for casing had been rinsed with salted water and were now delicately pulled onto the nozzle of the stuffing machine, like a stocking about to be pulled up a leg, but still gathered around the ankle.

So far, the mud pies had been fun and easy. I turned on the machine. As the meat began to emerge from the nozzle and into the intestinal casing, the 'stocking' slipped off. I turned off the machine, pulled the thin, slightly off-putting skin back on. This time, enough meat pushed through to twist the casing and give the sausage its shape. More meat pushed out and the weight pulled the skin off once again. By one in the morning I was in tears, in a very bad mood, hating babies, husbands and the nostalgia for English food. Miles took over. I washed up the dinner plates we had forgotten in the rush to begin.

Since then, the system has changed. I shape the mixture into sausage shapes, cook them without skins, or shape the meat in small ovals and wrap them in caul fat which melts during the frying.

From those days comes Pea Pond Pudding, in reality taken nearly exactly from a recipe of Jane Grigson which followed us to Beaver Dam. The repertory grew and grew, as I did – poires au cassis; chocolate truffles; little green gnocchi, delicate and speckled; bacalhau; brandade de morue. And Georgia, our second daughter, was born a month later, on 18 December, at one on a Saturday morning, just in time for her father's birthday.

Seven months later, on yet another record-breaking heat wave in July, we moved to Beaver Dam, a large one-storied house we rented for the next eight years. It stood on eighty acres of wooded land which opened up into spaces named by the children 'our secret fields'. One side of the house looked down on the stream that was indeed dammed by beavers. The huge glass windows of the sitting room were shaded by beech and fir trees and the room, in summer, was cooled by the power of suggestion of cold rushing water below. The other side of the house looked out on unmanicured paddocks sloping up to the woods. There was a pond on those grounds too, but out of sight of the house where, in April of each year, the same grey heron stayed for a few days, standing on top of the willow tree, perhaps on his way to Florida. In this house, I cooked Harrington's Ham, a discovery from Vermont. It was simply the best we would ever taste; as were those years.

Pea Pond Sausages

12oz / 350g lean VEAL, 1lb / 450g lean PORK, 8oz / 225g fat

back of pork, 1 slice of WHITE BREAD, 6 CLOVES, 1 table-spoon crushed BLACK PEPPER, ½ teaspoon each of CINNAMON, freshly grated NUTMEG, medium sweet PAPRIKA, ground CUMIN, a pinch of SUGAR, SALTPETRE and CAYENNE; PARSLEY, 1 teaspoon chopped GARLIC, 4 tablespoons RED WINE, 1 EGG.

Put the meats and fat back through the mincer twice, once using the coarse blade and once the finer blade. Using your hands mix the meats well with all the spices, the slice of bread (crust removed) soaked in the red wine, the beaten egg, parsley and garlic.

I sometimes vary this by reducing to a few tablespoonfuls a glass of RED WINE with CINZANO, a dash of CREAM, SHALLOTS, LEMON RIND and JUICE, soaking the bread in this reduction.

Shape the mixture into one long and fat sausage. Wrap in doubled cheesecloth that is lightly oiled; tie the ends and simmer the sausage for 30 minutes in red wine, or until it reaches a temperature of 160°C / 320°F. cool, remove cheesecloth and chill. Wrap in a brioche dough and bake in a medium hot oven for 40 minutes. Or serve as is, sliced.

Or, and this is what reduced me to tears the first time, being rather clumsy at that sort of thing years ago, stuff the sausage meat into washed intestinal skins, firmly and evenly, twisting every 3–4in / 7.5–10cm. Now, instead, I use crépinettes or caul fat, making small round cakes and easily wrapping each one in the delicate veil of fat. Then fry gently in butter, browning each side. I usually serve the sausages or crépinettes with caramelised sauce of TOMATOES, ONIONS and GARLIC; or APPLES stewed with ONIONS and CUMIN or CARAWAY SEEDS; or an ONION MARMALADE (see page 14); or STRING BEANS with turnipped PEARS (see page 6).

Pea Pond Pudding

This recipe comes from a book of Jane Grigson's and only varies from hers a little. The association with the view of Pea Pond in winter is so strong that I think of it as my own, as do friends who shared the pudding. I use dark brown sugar instead of white and, being unprofessional, my pastry is seldom perfectly joined. This results in some of the liquid slipping through and making the outside of the pudding nicely sticky. The following quantities are enough for four very greedy people or six more polite people. It should be eaten immediately after it is lifted from its steaming bath, not, as we once discovered, removed and kept warm, as it then deflates.

Mix 8oz / 200g of WHITE FLOUR with 4oz / 100g of fresh, chopped SUET. Make this into a softish dough with a little MILK and water. Roll into a circle, cut out a quarter for the lid. Set aside. BUTTER a 2½ pt / 1.25l pudding bowl generously. Put in the pastry, lifting the sides against the side of the bowl and close the cut out section by pinching. Stretch the pastry near to the top of the bowl. Put in 2oz / 50g of salted BUTTER, in pieces, with 3oz / 75g of dark brown SUGAR. Prick a thin-skinned LEMON well, with a thick needle or skewer, and place on the brown sugar. Sprinkle the lemon with another 3oz / 75g of brown SUGAR and 2oz / 50g of BUTTER.

Roll out the extra piece of pastry to make a lid, pressing and pinching the edges together. Pleat a large piece of foil over the pudding bowl and tie a strong cotton string around the top. Steam the pudding in simmering water that comes halfway up the bowl. Maintain that level during the cooking, for 3 to 4 hours, topping up with boiling water.

When ready, remove the bowl, then its foil cover and turn upside down onto a serving dish, first easing the sides from the bowl. A little of the brown sugar will ooze onto the dish, forming a delicious caramel-tasting pool of sauce, or pudding on Pea Pond, as we thought.

Little Green Gnocchi

Four of these gnocchi per person make a good starter. They look elegant and delicate on the plate but are greedily filling. More than four would be a mistake. They freeze well; remove them from the freezer in the morning and defrost gently in the fridge or cool place. This quantity will produce between 26 and 30 gnocchi, depending on the size you shape them into.

Bring a 10oz / 250g packet of FROZEN SPINACH to a simmer in a minute quantity of water, covered. Turn off the heat and leave to defrost. Drain thoroughly. In a mixing bowl, blend the 6oz / 150g RICOTTA with the 2 medium POTATOES, boiled and mashed. Add 1 lightly beaten EGG, 1 extra YOLK, 2oz / 45g white FLOUR, 5 tablespoons PARMESAN, ½ teaspoon grated NUTMEG, SALT, PEPPER and the cooled spinach. Mix well and leave to rest for an hour.

Have ready a large saucepan filled three quarters full with water. Bring to a boil, add SALT, bring down to a gentle simmer. Lightly flour a wooden board; make a little hill of flour on another board or plate. Using a tablespoon, scoop out a rounded helping of the gnocchi mixture, drop this into the hill of flour and gently scoop into the floured palm of your hand. Roll and toss the gnocchi as though it were a small crêpe and your flattened hand the frying pan, evenly distributing the flour coating all around it but also losing the excess.

Gently drop the gnocchi on the floured board, without pinching with your fingers. The mixture should take on, naturally, an oval shape as it rolls and falls, only a little bigger than a kumquat – about 2in / 5cm long and 1in / 2.5cm thick. When you have 6, drop them into the barely simmering water. They will start to rise to the surface within 20–40 seconds. Let them bob around for a minute and remove gently with a slotted spoon onto a doubled paper towel to drain. They will appear to have a slightly slimy coating of flour – don't worry, this disappears later.

When cooled, wrap the gnocchi individually in cling film for freezing. For serving, butter a gratin dish generously, lay the gnocchi on the bottom leaving a little space between each one, pour melted butter over them, cover with foil and bake for 10 minutes in a hot oven. Sprinkle with parsley and freshly grated Parmesan. As you serve, pour a spoonful of butter over each helping. This recipe is not as difficult as it sounds; it is rather fun playing with the delicate shapes and they are delicious.

Chocolate Truffles - Truffes de Beaver Dam

I started making these when long weekends got out of hand and I couldn't face making another tarte maison. They have now become a substitute for dessert. I am lazier these days and my tooth is less and less sweet. Passed around with a good bowl of fruit, though, there is a sense of dessert with home-made chocolate truffles. They freeze well and should be slowly de-frosted, in the fridge, during the day. This quantity will make between 30 and 40 truffles, which should take care of 4 dinner parties. My shaping is purposely uneven, keeping in mind the underground truffle they are named after, and somehow a perfectly round ball of chocolate is less satisfying.

Melt 10 oz / 250g of the best, dark, semi-sweet CHOCOLATE you can find, broken in small pieces, in the top of a covered double saucepan. Stir in, little by little, 3 oz / 75g of salted BUTTER, in pieces. When completely absorbed, remove from the heat, add 2 EGG YOLKS, stirring quickly, at the same time, with a wooden spoon. Add 1 tablespoon of instant COFFEE and 2 teaspoons of PEPPERMINT EXTRACT. Return to the double saucepan, above the simmering water, and stir for one or two minutes – until blood warm. Remove and place over a bowl of iced water, with ice cubes still floating about. Stir until cooled and beginning to harden around the edges of the pot. Refrigerate for at least 2 hours, or even overnight if you are busy.

Using a teaspoon, scoop out small amounts of the chocolate mixture onto a plate. When you have a dozen or so, shape into small uneven balls slightly larger than a Muscat grape and roll in a bowl of good COCOA powder until completely coated. Repeat, occasionally cooling your hands under cold water, and store in a jar for freezing.

I sometimes use ¼ teaspoon of finely grated ORANGE PEEL, instead of peppermint extract. The chocolate I mostly use is Menier or Lindt. The best, if you can find it, unusually high in cacao solids (61% – the average being under 40%), is called Valrhona. The cocoa powder I prefer is unsweetened and from Holland.

Women, while under the influence of the lunar cycle, should not cook eggs . . . an old wives tale I have discovered to be true on three occasions where I ended up with a curdled mess.

Bacalhau with Olives and Pine Nuts

If you are able to find salt cod that is not dried pancake-thin, with only a few bones and without fins, then prepare this recipe which is good and satisfying at any time of year.

1lb / 450g DRIED SALT COD, soaked overnight, rinsed under cold water several times; FLOUR for dusting; 6–8 tablespoons strong green OLIVE OIL; 1 large ONION, finely chopped; 4 GARLIC cloves, finely chopped; 1 14oz / 400g tin Italian PLUM TOMATOES; handful each of Niçoise BLACK OLIVES, CUR-RANTS and PINE NUTS; generous glass of dryish WHITE WINE; 2 broken BAY LEAVES; ½ teaspoon each of CAYENNE, ALLSPICE, FENNEL SEEDS, CHINESE FIVE SPICES; coarsely ground PEPPER.

Drain the soaked fish, pat dry and remove any skin or bones. Cut into bite-sized pieces, up to 2in/5cm. Dust with flour and fry in batches in a large pan, heated with enough olive oil to cover the bottom. When a deep golden brown, remove to drain on a paper towel. Arrange in a large, shallow gratin dish.

To the same frying pan, add a few more tablespoons of the olive oil and cook the onion and garlic for a few minutes until softened and just beginning to turn colour. Add the tomatoes, currants, white wine, bay leaves and spices. Simmer and stir for 15 minutes or until reduced by almost half. Pour over the fish, sprinkle with the olives and pine nuts. Bake in a medium hot oven for half an hour, checking the level of the sauce. Add a little wine if necessary. The dish should be moist, not quite liquid.

This will be even better the next day, reheated for just a brief quarter of an hour. Also good cold, with an AÏOLI or ROUILLE.

February

... a tiny man's coat that
kept appearing whenever she
moved house ...

Lino explores London; Toby comes for dinner

Lino explored London in hesitant English. At 5:30 in the morning he went to Bermondsey market. In the evening, understanding that the pub was England's bistro and café terrace, he took in two or three at a time. He went to the races, of dogs and horses, and watched snooker on the television. And I began to understand London better, through the eyes and voice of a foreigner more foreign than I.

Toby came for dinner, as he often did, on his way to the country on a Friday evening. This old friend told me I was a brave and lovely woman. It is at times like that, or when someone asks you grave questions, that you muse on how dirty the windows are. Compliments, under stress, are even harder to accept with grace, let alone credulity. I concentrated on trivia as the knots of divorce tightened. It was soon time for Toby to leave for New Mexico, or the Middle East, or the Sahara, as he usually did in the spring of each year I have known him. We didn't discuss the need for solitude. Instead, he told me he was ready for a wife, but that she was difficult to find. I wondered who would put up with his anti-clockwise travels. Against that, he was a man showing kindness and patience, whose laughter grew quieter over the years. A nervously warm and emotionally shy person to whom I wished much success. Months later, when he found the elusive woman, he told me that the problem with being in love is that you only want to be with that person. All others are irritants. I wondered if she lived up to his description of a 'dark and delicate beauty'. Toby's taste in women had been pungent, strong and exotic.

And Toby loves stews. I prepared three fillets of pork, a cut of meat that is reasonable here and, if obtainable in America, expensive. I sliced the sausage-shaped fillet into thick rounds. I browned the meat and softened chopped onion and fennel in its scrapings, then submerged it all in Marsala and white wine, thickening this liquid with Dijon mustard and olive paste. Then a dash of vinegar and to correct the slight bitterness of black olives, a tablespoon of maple syrup. Its nuttyness works better than the one-sided character of refined sugar. There were lentils to go with the meat, brought from France, smaller and firmer than lentils available in London and, I knew, another favourite of Toby's. They were from the same batch Giovanna and Lino had eaten, hoping for luck and peace. During dinner, Toby talked to the children about fishing, explaining to them the relation of flies to the time of day and weather. He reminded me of that small book, *The Spawning Run,* by a client of his, William Humphrey. A gentle parallel is drawn between the courtships of people and that of the salmon. A fishmonger in La Rochelle had once said to me: 'C'est le roi des poissons. Il meurt pour l'amour – mais les hommes et les chats survivent.'

Sometimes Toby drops in on Sunday evenings, this time on his way into town, with a freckled and wild trout, or its maligned cousin, the grayling. Their flesh would be firm and sweet. I appreciated both equally – baked, or dusted lightly in flour mixed with salt and pepper, then cooked in a little butter and peanut oil. I toast a few almonds in fresh butter, adding lemon juice and pour this over the fish when serving. With freshwater fish I like fennel. Its slight anise taste is reminiscent of clear sweet water. Or beetroot, if small and available uncooked at the market, which is irritatingly scarce unless ordered in advance. I boil them in the usual way, removing them while still firm, then peel and cut in half, warm them up again in just a teaspoon of butter with coarsely crushed peppercorns. Or stew them with onions and cumin, or ginger.

A *Stew for Toby*

The children, Toby and I had this with lentils and grilled tomatoes.

Slice 3 FILLETS OF PORK into thick rounds. Brown evenly at high heat, on all sides, in batches, using a generous quantity of OLIVE OIL and BUTTER. Set meat aside.

Discard any burnt fat, add fresh olive oil. Stir in 2 chopped ONIONS and 2 sliced bulbs of FENNEL. Cook 3–4 minutes, scraping up browned solids with the liquid escaping the vegetables. Return the meat, almost cover with a slightly dry WHITE WINE and a glass of BOURBON, diluted with one tablespoon of hot Dijon MUSTARD and OLIVE PASTE; a pinch of CHINESE FIVE SPICES, a teaspoon of cider or good sherry VINEGAR, a tablespoon of MAPLE SYRUP – it has more character than refined sugar, a nut-like caramel taste that balances the slight bitterness of the black olive paste. Simmer, covered for half an hour, then a few minutes uncovered to reduce the sauce. Taste for seasoning, add freshly ground PEPPER and chopped PARSLEY before serving.

Hot Beetroot

This vegetable is seldom served hot – a shame, as its character is more definite. I particularly like it with good, fresh fish. If you can find it uncooked at the market blanch 2–3 small BEETROOT per person, depending on their size, for a few minutes. Tested with a knife, they should feel like a slightly undercooked potato.

Remove, peel and return, halved, to a pan with melted butter. Stew gently, covered, with strips of fresh GINGER or 2–3 pinches of CUMIN or CARAWAY SEEDS, the squeeze of a LEMON, SALT and coarsely ground PEPPER, for 5 minutes or until just tender but not mushy.

Braised Fennel

Trim 1 small to medium bulb of FENNEL per person, shortening the stalks. Cut in half. Cook flat side down for a few minutes in sizzling BUTTER (not oil) in a shallow gratin dish so that the bottom of the bulb browns a little. Remove excess burnt butter, add a fresh knob. Sprinkle SALT, freshly ground PEPPER and 2 pinches of GROUND FENNEL onto the bulbs. Add a pinch of SUGAR and a small glass of dry WHITE WINE – or for a change MARSALA. Cook 10 minutes longer or until the bulb feels almost soft to the point of a knife but still a little firm. Serve in its dish, with freshly chopped PARSLEY and just a squeeze of LEMON JUICE.

If the following course is lean, I sometimes add a little single cream at the end. I particularly like the taste of fennel with freshwater fish.

Poires au Cassis

The cassis makes all the difference to this dessert. It is worth using one of good quality with a fairly high alcoholic content. In summer, a few scattered black or red currants add to the complexity and appeal.

Simmer for thirty minutes 16 fl oz / 500ml water with half a bottle of robust RED WINE, 2 glasses of CRÈME DE CASSIS, 4oz / 100g SUGAR, ½ teaspoon each of CINNAMON, NUTMEG (freshly grated), ALLSPICE; 1 tablespoon VANILLA

ESSENCE, 2 tablespoons ROSEWATER, 1 strip of ORANGE PEEL, 2 crushed BAY LEAVES; 1 tablespoon REDCURRANT JELLY.

Peel 1 PEAR per person and cut a slice from the bottom of each so that they stand upright. Leave on the stalk. Simmer the pears, covered, in the above syrup for 10–20 minutes, depending on ripeness and variety. I choose slightly unripe pears. Turn the pears once or twice so that they colour evenly.

Remove the fruit to a deep serving bowl. Taste the syrup and adjust the sweetness to your taste. Reduce a little further if it hasn't reached a pleasing syrupy thickness (it will thicken slightly when cold). Strain over the pears and refrigerate for several hours. Serve with double cream or crème fraîche, spiked with a little vanilla and dark rum, or the sauce sabayonnée (see page 6).

Flu; dreaming; mystery of tiny coat; Somerset friends

For two or three weeks, the children and I were anti-social. I was recovering from several days in bed with a temperature. I hadn't been bedridden in years, it felt uncomfortable, nor had I ever had a real bout with flu, a term so often used for a bad cold, but quite different, as I discovered. It seemed to bring with it days that lingered with heaviness of spirit and thought. Music, or a pretty view, made no impression at all. For two days, Gerry, our shy and grey-haired builder, arrived early enough at the house to take Georgia to school. In the afternoon I talked myself out of bed to fetch her and a little later, prepare dinner. I didn't feel like meat. On one of those evenings, I made a vegetable stew of courgettes, potatoes, string beans, cauliflower and peas, starting with onions melted in a light olive oil. My father called from Los Angeles knowing good news lifts the spirit. He told me a dirty joke, then that a bank, at long last, was backing his new venture. The loan had just been granted: 'I'm on my way there,' he said, laughing, 'in a van . . . it's going to be a hit and run job – they won't even have time to see my signature.' I felt better. Then my mother called. She told me a story about a tiny man's coat that kept appearing whenever she moved house. So tiny it could only belong to a lover the size of a mouse, but whose? She had been sorting out cupboards, now that she had decided to move back to

England. She described the coat further. Neat collar made of velvet, a handsome deep grey. A lawyer perhaps? We were getting giddy and incoherent, so we hung up.

Feeling even better now, I quartered and peeled a few potatoes, rolled them in the oil with cumin seeds. Then I added chicken stock and sliced courgettes. The children topped and tailed string beans alongside homework. Those went into the broth. Finally, a handful of peas. By then, probably forty five minutes in total, the liquid had taken on the taste of vegetables and thickened just enough. At table, we sprinkled parsley onto our dish and dribbled two or three drops of olive oil from the blue pottery jug. Now, a year later, I am sitting at the same table in a different house. At the other end, my nine-year-old Georgia is eating bread with Boursin, cucumbers and sticks of raw carrot, reading quietly a book about a mad crow. Between us, holding flowers instead of oil, is the same blue pot, bought several years ago in New Mexico. I remember the Indian leaning against an adobe wall, who explained that all those ladders I noticed by each dwelling were there to make it easy to reach the roof, to rest and dream – a daily need which I was forgetting to observe.

We ate our vegetable stew with a warm baguette I had bought in the morning. I had had a similar stew in Somerset, with David and Georgia, in their house that is a twelfth-century priory. We picked young broad beans and, once cooked, removed their skins. Being so young, the skins were almost as tender as the little bodies inside. Hungry, I seasoned them with coarse salt, pepper and olive oil and ate them. A lovely teaser, but only this way, while talking, laying the table, peeling potatoes. Georgia grows, tends, cooks her own vegetables and fruit. She shears and butchers her own sheep. Twelve, fourteen, sixteen people may appear for Sunday lunch. Four or ten may stay for the weekend. Georgia is small and brisk and striking. Her frame seems tiny against the shape of her daily work and I wonder how she does it without crushing in on herself. Her skill with food is truly breathtaking, without fuss.

Flu days passed. I introduced Lino to Toby, David and Georgia. It was immediately a dinner of friends. None have seen him since and all enquire after him, as he does after them. We had a poule au pot. One week, I roast a chicken. The next day, the carcass and bits of leftover meat make a stock, which I prefer to that made from uncooked fresh meat and bones. I freeze my stock and a week or two later use it for risotto or, this time, to simmer the poule with vegetables. Occasionally I use some of the winy stock produced by cooking a saucisson de Toulouse, to give the poule a double broth to accompany it.

Chicken and More Chicken

To start with the breasts, here are just a few of the endless ways of cooking them.

Cook the BREASTS (wings removed) on both sides in PEANUT OIL until lightly browned. Remove, pour off excess burnt fat. Add a little fresh BUTTER and OLIVE OIL. Warm a tablespoon of CUMIN SEEDS in the oil and butter. As they begin to sizzle, return the breasts to the pan, add a mixed handful of GREEN and BLACK OLIVES. Pour in a small glass of WHITE WINE, scrape up the browned solids. Add a few drops of PERNOD. Cover and simmer over a low heat for 15–20 minutes. Add a little more wine or stock if necessary, just to keep the breasts moist. There should be enough to spoon a few table-spoonfuls onto each breast when serving. Don't try to increase the sauce more than this or its essence will be lost. Serve with chopped fresh PARSLEY, freshly ground PEPPER, a little SALT to taste.

Or, brown the breasts in butter and HAZELNUT OIL (huile de noisettes). Separately, toast a few skinned HAZELNUTS in a few drops of the same oil; add these to the browned breasts with a few MUSCAT RAISINS, ½ teaspoon of CINNAMON, some ALLSPICE, a few CLOVES. Deglaze with a glass of medium dry WHITE WINE and a small glass of MARSALA. Cook, covered as above.

Or, brown the chicken breasts with 3 slices of LEMON for each and 1in / 2.5cm of fresh GINGER, peeled and slivered. Deglaze with a glass of WHITE WINE and a little STOCK. Simmer, covered, as above, with 2 tablespoons of freshly chopped ROSEMARY.

Or, if you have any left-over FLAGEOLETS or other cooked BEANS, purée a few tablespoons of the beans and use as a thickener for a sauce of WHITE WINE, VERMOUTH and a good pinch of SAFFRON.

Or, toast a few halved ALMONDS in ALMOND OIL. Add to the chicken breasts with 2 tablespoons of CORIANDER SEEDS, ½ teaspoon of PAPRIKA, 1 tablespoon of TOMATO PURÉE diluted with a glass of WHITE WINE and a glass of MADEIRA.

All the above sauces are enhanced with the addition of leftover gravies and a few tablespoons of stock. If you happen to have an unfinished bottle of a Bourgogne Aligoté, use this for the wine in the recipe with flageolets. Its almost smoky taste is interesting.

Grilling   Marinate the breasts for a few hours or all day in SESAME SEED OIL, a small glass of RED WINE diluted with 2 tablespoons of hot Dijon MUSTARD, 1 tablespoon TOMATO PURÉE, a generous sprinkle of SOY, TABASCO and WORCES-TERSHIRE SAUCE; 1 teaspoon of CUMIN or CORIANDER SEEDS depending on your inclination that day.

Place the chicken breasts in a shallow gratin dish, lightly oiled, marinade kept aside. Grill the underside first for 10 minutes, until well-browned. Turn over, pour the marinade over the breasts, grill another 10–15 minutes, occasionally spooning the sauce over the browning breasts. If it thickens and caramelises too much, add a little MADEIRA.

Roast Chicken

If at all possible, I will buy a 6lb / 2.7kg chicken, whether I am cooking for two, four or more. The leftovers provide another day or two for risotto or salads and soups. The carcass makes enough stock to last a while. I combine roasting with braising, endlessly varying the system. The size of the chicken means it cooks all the longer, allowing the sauce to develop further.

Heat the oven to hot. Rub the chicken with BUTTER, a little SALT and freshly ground PEPPER. Lay the bird on its side in a well-oiled roasting pan at least 1½in / 3–4cm deep. Bake 10 minutes and turn on to the other side. Bake a further 10 minutes. Redress the chicken, breast upright, remove excess melted fat, but leave two or three tablespoonfuls. Lower the heat to medium hot.

Add to the pan a mirepoix of CARROT, ONION, CELERY and MUSHROOM. Pour over the mirepoix two glasses of RED or WHITE WINE, scrape up the browned bits on the bottom of the pan, stir in 1 tablespoon of hot Dijon MUSTARD, 1 tablespoon of TOMATO PURÉE diluted with a little stock or water. Bake until the juices of the bird run clear, then leave to rest, oven door ajar, for ten minutes. Baste every 10 to 15 minutes, adding a little stock or wine as the sauce evaporates, thickens and starts to caramelise at the edge of the pan. Scrape off and incorporate the browned solids formed on the sides of the pan. The reason for not adding the liquid all at once is that the sauce must reduce and caramelise several times. This deepens and develops its taste.

Or, put slices of LEMON, LEMON PEEL and BAY LEAVES under the skin of the bird. Lay chopped pieces of PANCETTA or smoked BACON or HAM around the chicken. Use for the sauce 2 glasses of MADEIRA and a glass of dry VERMOUTH. Baste as usual, thickening if necessary with a little Dijon MUSTARD.

Or, dilute OLIVE PASTE with a few tablespoons of PERNOD, 2 glasses of white PORT, a little TOMATO PURÉE. Scatter a few green OLIVES and whole cloves of GARLIC around the bird.

Or, make a paste of a dozen ANCHOVIES, adding a few drops at a time of good SHERRY VINEGAR, then 2 glasses of WHITE WINE. Cook with whole cloves of GARLIC. As the chicken rests, sprinkle a generous quantity of fresh TARRAGON, chopped.

Une Poule au Pot

Cover a fine HEN or POULET DE BRESSE with chicken STOCK, a fruity WHITE WINE, a dash of mild VINEGAR and any LIQUOR left from a saucisson de Toulouse. Bring to a brisk simmer. Skim off the foam that will rise; add ½ teaspoon each of freshly grated NUTMEG, ALLSPICE, CHINESE FIVE SPICES. Add 5 or 6 whole, peeled, GARLIC cloves – or more, if you like garlic as much as I do (it becomes sweet when cooked in stock) – a few quartered ONIONS or whole small onions. Simmer gently, covered, for 20 minutes.

Add fresh vegetables, such as CARROTS, POTATOES, COURGETTES or STRING BEANS, depending on the market and mood. If using fine French string beans, add them during the last 5 minutes of cooking. Simmer uncovered another 20 minutes, or until the chicken, tested between thigh and body, appears to be ready. Remove the poule to a serving dish, carve, arrange the drained vegetables around it, cover with foil and keep warm in a very low oven.

Reduce the stock at a high boil and taste it for seasoning. Pour as is over meat and vegetables, or thicken with an EGG YOLK mixed with a little SINGLE CREAM. Sprinkle generously with finely chopped PARSLEY and a little fresh CORIANDER. Season with coarsely ground PEPPER.

Légumes au Pot Remonte-Pente

This is a cross between soup and stew, refreshing after a bout of low spirits or health. Choice of vegetables of course depends on mood and season; this is a rough guide:

In OLIVE OIL soften 2 large ONIONS, chopped, and 3–4 cloves GARLIC (if using whole cloves, put them in later with the stock). Add 2–3 waxy POTATOES, peeled and quartered, and cook a few minutes with 1 tablespoon of CUMIN or CARAWAY SEEDS. This brings out the taste of the seeds. Add 1 COUR-GETTE, unpeeled, cut into thick rounds, and a small handful of STRING BEANS. Cover with a strong CHICKEN BROTH, or pheasant if in season, and the juice of 1 LEMON. Simmer, uncovered, for 1–1½ hours. Fifteen minutes before serving, add the rest of the vegetables – 1 COURGETTE, another small handful of STRING BEANS, some PEAS. The broth will have thickened slightly and absorbed the taste of vegetables. Add freshly ground PEPPER and BASIL leaves.

At table, dribble a little fresh OLIVE OIL over your plate and perhaps add just a little grated PARMESAN.

If you use TOMATOES, peel them (I like the seeds, otherwise remove) and put them in at the beginning. CAULIFLOWER or BROCCOLI should go in during the last 15 minutes.

March

... a tall jar of olive oil which
held within its scent a feeling of
Mont Ventoux like a ship in a bottle...

At home in London; a visit from Provence

Walking in the rain along Ebury Street where I had picked up warm petits pains au chocolat for tea – the children's favourite – I was crossed by a form teacher making the tail of a crocodile of small boys wearing a uniform of bright yellow sweater and grey shorts. 'Make sure your socks are pulled up, please.' Scene and sentence seemed so terribly English. I thought of other English things, remembering first the phrase 'a grey, grim pavement of a day, with slow dropping rain . . .' Box hedges, potted shrimp, I continued to myself; the quality of an English spring, the sense of wading through blossom; the painter who walked in yesterday, looking down at the cat sitting by the front door: 'Hullo puss, how are you?' in a polite and conversational tone, showing teeth like old teapots; the ambivalent curiosity towards foreigners; front gardens, such brightly painted front doors leading to subdued interiors; the horse and carriage of Young's Brewery passing through London and modern age without stopping for red lights – no one seems to object.

This was my second year in London. It was becoming, at last, home. I'd had lunch with my mother who had returned a few days before from Provence. She brought honey from her village with the same instructions as last time: 'Wait for two or three weeks. It has just been potted. It will thicken.' The anticipation grew as the honey settled. And a tall jar of olive oil which held within its scent a feeling of Mont Ventoux, like a ship in a bottle. Lunch was simple. A smoked magret de canard from my French butcher and, out of curiosity, smoked lamb from Cumberland called Macon. Both would keep at least two weeks and, though extravagant, would stretch. We started with a few thin slivers of the duck and its skin, smoky and peppery, barely touched by olive oil I had scented with a truffle. Then a salad of frisée, fresh tarragon, burnt yellow peppers. A well-aged farmhouse Cheddar. It was enough. We shared news of family, health, the dress my sister Georgia, just twenty, would wear to a ball that was a friend's 1940 Balenciaga; the Russian whose biography my mother was writing, pictures of Coco Chanel she might use in the book.

I dropped in on my mother the following week. She made her coffee that always tastes like it smells in Italian expresso bars. We dropped a thick teaspoon of cream into our cups and watched it rise up to the surface like Chinese water flowers. The phone rang. My stepfather, from Paris. They have been separated for possibly fifteen years. She hung up remarking his ego was so huge 'it blocks the view'. At lunch, we had poireaux à la coriandre, prepared the previous morning. It takes ten minutes to do, then a day's rest in its cooking liquid, with crushed coriander seeds and lemon juice, finishes the make-up. I brought the smoked lamb. We decided it was delicate and strange, uncertain whether we liked it or not. My mother was driving down to Sussex that afternoon to look for a house. We walked to her car. Her hand waved out the window like a brave and merry flag.

The telephone was getting to me. I decided to buy an answering machine. The next day, Lino came to help me choose. Then we celebrated this luxury over lunch. A pissaladière and a glass of red wine.

Poireaux à la Coriandre

Slice lengthwise young and small LEEKS, cleaned and rinsed, two per person. Sweat gently for 2 or 3 minutes in a light OLIVE OIL, flat side down, in a large enamel gratin dish. Before the leeks begin to stick or brown, add a few tablespoons of water or chicken STOCK (better, but don't use stock cubes). Cover and stew gently until they just start to wilt, about 3 to 4 minutes. Only 3 to 4 tablespoons of liquid should remain; if not, remove the leeks and reduce at a high temperature.

Cool, pour the cooking liquid over the leeks. Add to your taste fresh OLIVE OIL, LEMON JUICE (not vinegar), SALT and a thimble per person of crushed CORIANDER SEEDS, previously and briefly fried in a lightly oiled pan to bring out their taste. Refrigerate for at least a day, occasionally turning the leeks over in their dressing. Serve with freshly ground PEPPER and chopped PARSLEY and CHIVES.

Salade de Frisée, Poivrons Jaunes avec Estragon

Wilt and brown thin slices of YELLOW PEPPER in OLIVE OIL until almost crisp and near-burnt. You may find it difficult not to keep stirring the peppers to prevent them from burning, but the burnt taste is necessary.

Remove the excess burnt oil, if any. While the pan is still warm, but not hot, add VINEGAR and fresh OLIVE OIL, thickly ground PEPPER, a handful of fresh, chopped TARRAGON leaves. Pour this warm dressing and peppers over the FRISÉE LETTUCE. Serve immediately.

This is also good with leftover skin of chicken or duck, slowly crisped in a low oven for an hour or two.

Pissaladière

This is a Provençal version of pizza, delicious at any temperature. Warm or hot in winter; shade cool in summer. A light lunch, with a salad to follow perhaps. Travels well on a picnic.

The following proportions are for a tart 8in / 20cm in diameter and will feed 6 people. I use a tart tin with removable base, of dark metal, with fluted edges.

Make the pastry ahead of time, line the tin and keep in the fridge, an hour or a day. My choice of pastry varies, depending on mood and what I did the last time. Sometimes a pâte brisée for savouries or a cross between that and a pâte feuilletée which means rolling the pâte brisée three times, refrigerating between each folding and rolling.

A simple mixture is 6oz / 160g WHITE FLOUR, pinch SALT, 3oz / 80g BUTTER, 1 EGG. The pastry used in the tarte à la moutarde (page 40) recipe works equally well.

Warm a generous amount of strong OLIVE OIL and a knob of BUTTER in a large cast iron pan. Sweat 8 to 10 medium ONIONS, sliced, with 2 cloves of GARLIC, finely chopped. Cook gently with 2 broken BAY LEAVES, covered, for 1 hour. Stir occasionally. Remove the lid and cook gently another 45 minutes to 1 hour. They will at first shrink to half and be quite wet. Uncovered they will shrink further, you will need to stir often to prevent them from sticking to the point of burning. At the end you will have a sort of jam or purée of onion, sweet and caramelised. The colour should be a soft ochre. Remove the bay leaves. Tip the pan to one side and push the onions to the high side. At least 2 tablespoons of oil and butter will ooze down the pan. Remove the onions, keep the oil and butter for frying an egg, set the onion marmalade aside. Usually I need a good 6 tablespoons of olive oil and 1 or 2 tablespoons of butter.

While the onions cook, prepare a TOMATO SAUCE: simmer

6oz / 140g Italian TOMATO PURÉE with approximately 10 fl oz / 300ml of good CHICKEN STOCK (or water, but not stock cubes), 1 BOUQUET GARNI, a dash of CAYENNE and SUGAR, 1 or 2 tablespoons of your morning COFFEE (this cuts the acidity) or 1 tablespoon of instant coffee. Simmer, uncovered, 25–30 minutes. The sauce should reduce to the consistency of runny ketchup.

These two sauces can be made a day or two ahead of time. When ready to cook the pissaladière, sprinkle a small handful of grated PARMESAN mixed with grated COMTÉ cheese on the bottom of the pastry case. Cover evenly with the onion purée (put down in big spoonfuls over the cheese, then spread each so as not to disturb the cheese underneath), then the tomato sauce. Cover lightly with another handful, generous this time, of the same two cheeses. Dot on as many tiny Niçoise black OLIVES as you like, in a nice pattern. Make a star in the centre with a few ANCHOVIES. Bake half an hour in a hot oven, lower shelf. Leave to rest at least 10 to 15 minutes.

Sardo cheese is as good as Comté for this tart.

Tarte à la Moutarde, Tomates Cerises

I call this a tart rather than a quiche as the custard is much firmer and because it is not so deep. It is quite spicy, the mustard used being Dijon à l'ancienne (better than Meaux) which has the seeds. The cumin seeds give it an unexpected taste which goes well with cheese. I use a tart tin, of dark metal, with a removable base and fluted edges, about 10in / 25cm in diameter. The tart will serve 6 to 8 people. It is equally good hot, after a few minutes' rest, or cool.

Make a pastry with 4½oz / 110g BUTTER, 10oz / 250g WHITE FLOUR, 1 beaten EGG, 3 tablespoons WHITE WINE, 1 tablespoon OLIVE OIL, a dash of SALT, and crushed PEPPER-CORNS if you want to increase the spiciness. Line the tin and let the pastry rest for an hour in the fridge or cool place. This is my version of a Simca recipe. Smooth 3 heaped tablespoons of Dijon MUSTARD à l'ancienne over the pastry. Sprinkle on a small handful of grated COMTÉ CHEESE, prick the pastry and bake blind for about 10 minutes in a medium oven – if too hot, the pastry may rise in irritating bubbles.

Beat lightly 2 EGGS plus one YOLK, 11 fl oz / 350ml single CREAM, 2 heaped tablespoons of the same mustard, another handful of the grated Comté cheese, and 3 tablespoons of grated PECORINO. Set aside.

Quickly fry one medium ONION, finely sliced, in OLIVE OIL, so that the exterior is near-burnt but the interior slightly uncooked. Dot the pastry case with 8 to 10 CHERRY TOMATOES, cut in half, cut side up; place a few whole ones around the edges of the tart. Pour the cream mixture over the tomatoes. Sprinkle with 1 tablespoon of CUMIN SEEDS and the burnt onion. Bake in a medium hot oven, on the lower shelf, for 15 to 20 minutes, or until it is set but not solid (it will set further when cooling), and the top is well browned. Let rest a few minutes before serving.

If you cannot find cherry tomatoes, omit the tomatoes altogether. If you want an even firmer texture for the custard, when beating the eggs add a heaped tablespoon of white FLOUR.

La Smala in St. Barthélémy; cooking and exploring; poisonous fish

It seems a March years and years ago that we went to St. Barthélémy, a French island in the Caribbean. Miles and the girls protected their tissue paper skins by wearing caftans under the sun and I thought of them as my pale Arab family – 'la smala' as the Arabs say, a term that gathers all family creatures under one wing including hens and goats. We lived in two bedrooms, one step above the sand and forty paces from the sea, with a sitting room that was a wide terrace, and an open kitchen on the side. Bread was imported from another island on a twin prop Cessna. I bought baguettes from a pilot who stood, in shorts and khaki shirt, on the vaguely tarred runway by the airport hut. Fish came from the old man who stood on the quay of Gustavia, the main port, early in the morning and sometimes just before sunset. He told me of the island's copper deposits. Fish that swam on the south and west sides of the island were poisonous, even deadly. 'Never eat,' he said, 'Fausse Carangue or Almaco Jack; Aigrette – it looks like a hog with antennae; or Capitaine Z'Ailes Jaunes, the Yellowfish Grouper.' Possible, but risky, were the Coffre Zinga (Spotted Trunkfish), always bootfaced; or the Coffre Rond (Smooth Trunkfish) with giraffe markings. But he assured me the Spanish Mackerel and the Soleil in his bag would be safely delicious.

Fresh herbs and lettuce were impossible to find, until our third day, exploring the island, we drove past a small, neatly tended vegetable patch, a sight difficult to miss in the middle of the scruffy mass of tropical shrubs and palm trees. A bare-footed Breton woman appeared at the doorway of her tin-roofed shack, wearing an old and clean black dress, with white lace cap and apron as fresh as a postcard, her skin the texture of tree trunks. I bought parsley, chives, rosemary, thyme and small heads of lettuce. We drove back to our bay in the car that was really a toy on wheels, without windows or doors, the roof a flapping awning. The smell of fresh, wet, green things on my lap made me feel absurdly prosperous. We ate most evenings a fish cooked over onions and tomatoes, eggplant and garlic – steaming and absorbing the taste of vegetables underneath, with an occasional sprinkle of Pernod or allspice. Equipment was minimal: two frying pans, one large, one small; one saucepan, plates and two bowls, a few glasses reduced to fewer by the time I filled two or three with precious herbs, and branches of the tropical variety of Impatiens that grew in the sand by the back door; two good knives and a peppermill, brought from home. Cooking was shaped accordingly and seemed an achievement. I continued to cook fish this way back in Beaver Dam but without the same satisfaction. We bought fruit twice a week from fat women on the beach, who looked exactly like the rag doll on my bathroom windowsill here in Fulham, and allspice berries and chilli peppers. We returned three times to the island during our decade in the States, but the description I have heard recently no longer fits my memory of it. I don't expect to see it again, nor do I want to.

Kingfish Steaks, with Mustard and Vinegar

Other fish that suit this dish are haddock, hake, swordfish, monkfish and turbot.

I became very fond of kingfish in New York; it is low in fat, its texture a little like that of mullet crossed with cod. It takes well to this sauce.

Melt a few tablespoons of sweet BUTTER with chopped ONION and GARLIC, about 3 medium onions and 2 cloves of garlic. Add a teaspoon of mild VINEGAR per steak. Wilt the vegetables for a few minutes but don't let them burn. Lay the fish steaks over the mixture, add just enough WHITE WINE to create steam. Cover and cook for 4 to 5 minutes on each side, depending on the thickness of the steak — it should be at least three quarters of an inch/15mm.

Remove the fish, mix 3 tablespoons of Dijon MUSTARD into the pan with the onions, and add half a glass of WHITE WINE or SHERRY. Reduce until syrupy, return the fish, cover, leave to rest another minute, heat turned off.

Serve with chopped PARSLEY mixed with 1/2 teaspoon of finely grated LEMON PEEL and coarsely ground PEPPER. I leave salt to be added at table. Used during the cooking, it seems to detract from the sweetness of the fish.

It is preferable to undercook the fish. When you return it to the reduced sauce it will finish cooking in the heat, so leaving it to rest will not overcook it.

Bourride of Scallops or Small Fish Stew

Have ready approximately 2 pints / 1 litre of reduced and strained FISH STOCK (see recipe). This allows 2 ladlefuls of stock per person. The following will feed four people.

Bring the stock to a gentle simmer. Add 3 tablespoons each of finely julienned FENNEL, CELERY, CARROT and LEEK. Chop finely 3 or 4 SHALLOTS, add to the stock. Simmer five minutes.

Put 2lb / 900g SCALLOPS into the stock and simmer for 2 to 3 minutes. Remove the pot from the heat. Using a slotted spoon, take out the scallops and vegetables. Place decoratively on a serving dish, cover and keep warm in a gentle oven.

Stir a few tablespoons of single CREAM mixed with 2 EGG YOLKS into the stock, whisking rapidly. Reheat the stock, whisking, until it is near the point of simmering. Strain over the scallops, reserving a little for second helpings. Serve with CROÛTONS, fresh PARSLEY and AÏOLI on the side.

If you are anywhere near Long Island, New York, treat yourself to the bay scallops. Only cook them for 1 minute.

For a FISH STEW, add to the stock above 1lb / 450g of perfect, waxy, tiny NEW POTATOES. When they are cooked, add 1½lb / 625g of fish steaks or fillets such as MONKFISH, HALIBUT, MULLET or BASS. Omit the cream and egg yolks. Cook the fish for 5 minutes in the stock. Serve directly from the pot with a ladle of stock over each portion of fish. Have on the table the AÏOLI or ROUILLE.

Aubergines with Feta

This can be done several hours ahead of time; it is the sort of meal that makes me smile, much more than the best three-star lunch in a cool and elegant restaurant.

Slice an unpeeled AUBERGINE into ½in / 1cm thick rounds. Fry the slices in batches, in OLIVE OIL, until a deep tobacco colour on both sides. Remove with a slotted spoon to drain on paper towels. When all the slices are done, cook thin slices of fresh GARLIC in fresh olive oil, in the same pan. Remove and deglaze the pan, scraping up the browned solids, adding 3 tablespoons of a good SHERRY or CIDER VINEGAR and 2 tablespoons of dry WHITE WINE.

Arrange the aubergines in an oval serving dish, and scatter over the garlic pieces. Pour on the vinegar and white wine; sprinkle a handful of Feta CHEESE over and around the vegetables, dribble on a few tablespoons of dark green OLIVE OIL; then add freshly and coarsely ground PEPPER, SALT and any fresh HERBS available – BASIL or MINT being the best. A few Niçoise BLACK OLIVES around the edges and a few slices of SALAMI or ANCHOVIES will make this into a complete hors d'oeuvres or a summer lunch.

Aubergines Basquaises

Goose fat is the scent of Basque kitchens, and it is now fairly easy to obtain in tins imported from France. Once opened, transfer to a glass jar and refrigerate. It will keep well for a couple of months. Or, if you have recently cooked a goose, keep the fat and little brown scrapings and use this instead.

Slice 2 medium unpeeled AUBERGINES into ½in / 1cm thick rounds. Fry a few slices at a time, depending on the size of your frying pan, in a generous quantity of GOOSE FAT. You will need to keep adding fat as the aubergines absorb an amazing amount within seconds. Cook the slices until they are a deep tobacco colour on both sides. Remove with a slotted spoon to paper towels to drain. Continue until all the aubergines are done. Line a large, shallow gratin dish with them. There will be no need to grease the dish as the aubergines will release more juice and oils as they cook later in the oven.

Remove any burnt fat, and add fresh goose fat to the frying pan. Fry 1 large ONION, chopped finely, with 4 cloves of GARLIC, finely chopped, until softened. Scatter over the aubergines. Slice 2 sweet RED PEPPERS, lengthwise and cook in the same way, but let them burn a little. Arrange along the sides of the gratin dish.

Slice a CHORIZO SAUSAGE on the bias and fry briefly at high heat to seal and brown. Lay the chorizo pieces over the onion and aubergine, leaving the red line of peppers intact.

All this can be done well ahead of time. Twenty minutes before serving, bake in a hot oven for 10 minutes or until the edges of the vegetables start to caramelise. Leave to rest another 10 minutes in the oven, heat turned off, door left ajar. Sprinkle with freshly ground PEPPER and PARSLEY. This will serve 4 to 6 people, even 8 if this is an accompaniment to other vegetables and meats at a buffet.

Or, omit the sausage and lay fillets of fresh FISH on the vegetables. Cover lightly, cook until the fish is done in a hot oven or on top of the stove if your dish is an enamelled cast-iron pan. The fish will steam over the vegetables, absorbing their scent.

Saumon au Pernod

This is equally good with steaks of turbot, bass or halibut, but the scent of Pernod seems to marry particularly well with salmon. Ask your fishmonger to cut you steaks at least ¾in / 2cm thick. For two people, steaks weighing from 6–8oz / 150–200g each; colour a mirepoix of 1 ONION, 1 CARROT, 1 stick of CELERY or half a small bulb of FENNEL in BUTTER and HAZELNUT OIL until soft and golden. Deglaze with a small glass of PERNOD and a generous glass of fruity or near-sweet WHITE WINE. Lay the SALMON STEAKS over the moistened mirepoix.

Cover and steam the fish at a low heat for 5 minutes, depending on the thickness of the steaks. Serve each steak with a couple of spoonfuls of the mirepoix spread on top, and its

cooking liquor. Sprinkle with CHIVES and coarsely ground
PEPPER.

Should you have trouble finding Pernod, substitute with a glass
of WHITE PORT or MADEIRA and ½ teaspoon of ground
FENNEL or CHINESE FIVE SPICES.

Red Wine Sauce for Fish

This is simple to do, an elegant surprise. It has several sources – a
recipe of my father's, the once-in-a-while treat to an expensive
restaurant in France and reading books written by the masters of
cuisine nouvelle . . . an exception to my basic preference for un-
glossy food.

Ask your fishmonger to prepare fillets, skin removed, at least
¾in / 2cm thick, of BASS, MONKFISH, TURBOT or MULLET,
allowing 6–8oz / 150–200g per person for each fillet.

BUTTER an enamelled gratin dish generously. Lay the fillets
on the bottom. Choose your vegetable according to tempera-
ment, season and weather: either blanch for 1 minute in boiling
water, a sweet CABBAGE leaf for each fish fillet; or leaves of your
favourite LETTUCE, such as oak leaf (this particular one being
delicate should not be blanched). Prepare a julienne of LEEKS
and CARROTS with slivers of SHALLOTS, briefly wilted in
BUTTER.

Lay the julienne over the fish and then cover with the leaf
which will keep it moist. Pour over 2 generous glasses of RED
WINE such as a Médoc or Cahors and a small shot of dry
VERMOUTH. This is enough for four fillets. Break 2 BAY
LEAVES into the pool of red wine around the fish. Bake in a hot
oven for 5 minutes. Check that the fish is opaque, transfer the
sauce to a small saucepan while keeping the fish warm on a
serving dish. Reduce the sauce to a near-glaze, remove the bay
leaves and whisk in, little by little, 5 to 6 tablespoons of sweet
BUTTER and a squeeze of LEMON JUICE. Pour over the fish;
serve immediately with a grind of fresh PEPPER and finely
chopped PARSLEY.

For perfection, use a fine sieve to strain the sauce over the fish.
If, while being kept warm, the fish has released more liquid, blot
this up or spoon it into the sauce.

Brandade de Morue

This can be made ahead of time and will freeze well, in which case defrost it slowly in the fridge. Check the seasoning and, if necessary, whisk it to fluff it up as you re-heat it in a double boiler. It is rich, a little goes a long way, either as a starter or as a supper's main course followed by a salad. Serve on a slice of white bread fried in olive oil; surround with small Niçoise olives and sprinkle a generous amount of finely chopped fresh parsley.

Soak a 1lb / 450g piece of SALT COD overnight, rinsing several times in fresh water. Bring to the boil in a large saucepan filled with fresh water; remove after one minute. Drain, remove any skin and bones. Have ready approximately 12 fl oz / 350ml of a strong OLIVE OIL and the same quantity of MILK mixed with a little single CREAM. Both should be lukewarm to warm. The quantity will vary a little, according to the quality of the cod and your palate.

Cook 2 medium POTATOES, peel and reduce to a purée with a masher. Peel and crush at least 6 GARLIC cloves.

Using a bowl and whisk or a Magimix, shred the cod into the bowl, add the potatoes and garlic. Turn on the machine, dribble through the funnel alternately oil and cream-enriched milk. As the salt cod absorbs and swells, taste. At the end, add LEMON JUICE and coarsely ground PEPPER. The consistency should be that of a thick mousse. The taste is vividly Mediterranean.

Fish Stock

I make this once every two or three months and store it in various sizes of jam jars to use later for soup, fish stews and sauces. It freezes well. It will take a quarter of an hour of your time at various stages, adding up to a total, perhaps, of one hour, as it bubbles and simmers on its own. The house will be permeated that day by the smell, which is another reason to do it ahead of time, although I rather like the invisible invasion at the time. Just open the windows in the evening so that you don't wake up to it the next morning.

Use 2 large heads of FISH, avoiding salmon and mackerel, and any shells your fishmonger can provide you with, such as LOBSTER, CRAB, SHRIMP and LANGOUSTINE. Rinse well under running cold water and place heads and shells into a large stockpot. Cover with cold water, add ½ bottle of RED WINE, ½ bottle of WHITE WINE, 2 tablespoons of a mild VINEGAR. Bring to a boil, skim the froth that will rise. Simmer 45 minutes.

Remove the fish heads and shells; strain the stock into a clean pot. Add two 14oz / 400g tins of Italian PLUM TOMATOES; several shakes of SOY and TABASCO; a strip of ORANGE PEEL; 2 pinches of SAFFRON; 1 teaspoon each of ALLSPICE, GROUND FENNEL, and GROUND CUMIN; 1 tablespoon each of crushed CORIANDER SEEDS, PEPPERCORNS, CLOVES; a shot of PERNOD, GIN and BOURBON; 1 medium ONION, chopped; 4 or 5 cloves of GARLIC, chopped. Simmer for at least 4 hours. The stock should reduce by half and turn to an appealing earthy and copper colour. Strain and cool.

Spices and seasoning vary – add more wine to your taste, other vegetables, a little TOMATO PURÉE or OLIVE PASTE. The fish heads should weigh about 2lb / 900g each; leave 1 or 2 lobster shells during the second stage of the stock as they will continue to scent the liquor; remove the shells after another hour.

Caramelised Pineapple St. Barts

I started this by accident while we were holidaying at St. Barthélémy. It has remained a favourite of the children's and the rest of us.

Prepare the PINEAPPLE and slice into ¾in / 2cm thick rounds. Leave the centre core, as this holds the slice securely during the cooking; remove the core afterwards. Leave the pineapple rounds to drain in a colander, over a plate, to catch the juices.

Heat a few tablespoons of sweet BUTTER in a large frying pan. As it starts to sizzle, fry the pineapple rounds in batches of 4 or 5, depending on the size of your pan. There should be at least ½in / 1.25cm between each slice to prevent them from stewing in their own juices. Cook 2–3 minutes on each side at medium to high heat, until they brown quite deeply, which they will do unevenly. Add butter when necessary. Place each batch on a serving dish.

Pour out any excess burnt butter from the pan and add 2–3 knobs of fresh butter. As it melts and begins to bubble, add 4 tablespoons of WHITE SUGAR and 4 tablespoons of DARK

BROWN SUGAR with the collected juice from the draining pineapple slices. Scrape up the browned solids in the pan, add a little LEMON JUICE to taste, 2 glasses of sweet WHITE WINE or leftover CHAMPAGNE. As the sauce reduces, developing a caramel-like and syrupy texture, pour over the fruit. Arrange a few leaves of fresh MINT. Keep in a barely warm oven or, if you have made the dessert ahead of time, keep the ᴗauce separate, as the pineapple will continue to release excess juice which thins the caramel.

Soho; holiday under the sheets; mosquitoes and peppermills

Restless this particular day, I went up to Soho to buy food for dinner. On the way back, grumbling about grey pavement and grey sky and wet feet, craving a change of climate, I looked through a shop window at expensively plain, white cotton sheets, marked at half-price. Egyptian cotton; they would need ironing each week; even on sale they were extravagant. I shut my eyes, bought two pairs, rushed home, stripped my bed, and made it up again with the new pair of sheets and pillowcases, slid under the top sheet imagining the smell of just-washed laundry drying in the sun. I thought of summer, somewhere sometime and made myself a promise to find a space on my calendar for a week alone, beached and thoughtless. And so I did, but not alone.

I sit here, a year later, winding time backwards, remembering that day, under the sheets, able to tell the future. Off we would go, a few weeks later, to a friend's house on the Mediterranean. We walked to a small beach around the corner to have lunch beside a shack that looked like an old straw hat standing on stilts. We ate a fish called Pajero and drank what the unshaven fisherman and cook prepared for us: holding a bottle in each hand, he shook grand measures of each into a glass pitcher. First, brandy, then 'hierbas', translated on request as 'maybe absinthe, maybe anise'. Then pieces of orange, lemon, banana; finally, an afterthought for colour, red wine. This was called 'sangria'.

That evening, noticing stars and the smell of the sea, I put flowers on the table and made a ratatouille spicy enough to please a dragon (my companion liked to *inhale* pepper), doubling usual quantities of garlic and pimiento. On the side, a long and hot chorizo sausage, fresh bread, olive oil and the peppermill I travel with. And all was good.

On the third day of this holiday, my companion suggested a walk. He was bored with swimming. We drove to the other side of the island and parked by a café high above the sea. We started, through dry and thistly fields. After two hours, we stopped to eat our picnic. Mayonnaise, chorizo, tomatoes, hard-boiled eggs, olives, red wine, and the peppermill. We watched a lizard, then two, then three. The walk continued. I realized, after another hour, that this was to be serious exercise. I hadn't walked like this since I was twelve and wasn't certain of being up to it. I kept this to myself. Two or three hours later, around and down a mountain, we rested on a pebbled beach, staring at a huge rock on our left, rising interminably out of the sea. 'Verdad', someone said was its name. The next half hour felt impossible, as we started up again, but it passed. We reached the café by five in the afternoon, having started around ten. Within minutes, we had each drunk four glasses of fruit juice, two glasses of water, two glasses of beer. I was amazed at myself but said nothing, much too pleased.

We returned to London on a Sunday afternoon. I felt well and thought of stars and lizards while my dragon friend reminded me of mosquitoes, the fridge door that wouldn't shut or cool the beer, and the huge rock called Truth which I had completely forgotten.

This holiday was to come and pass, but that afternoon, after daydreaming under my new sheets, I dressed, went down to the kitchen and prepared dinner for myself and the children, cheered by my purchase. The results of shopping in Soho were on the table. Sesame oil, shrimp, ginger, scallions and sweet cabbage.

Ratatouille for a Dragon

My version of this dish is to cook each vegetable separately. The gratin dish is lined, bottom and sides, with aubergine. Then, in the middle, green and red and yellow peppers; around these, onions and garlic, then a circle of fiery tomatoes. You taste each separately as you eat them together.

I serve this often cold at dinner parties. The following recipe will be enough for sixteen, with other salads and meats.

Top and tail 2 large AUBERGINES; slice, unpeeled, in rounds 1/4–1/2in / 1cm thick. Cover the bottom of a large frying pan with 1/4in / 6mm of good OLIVE OIL. Fry a few slices of the aubergine at a time, at medium heat, adding more oil when necessary (they absorb, within seconds, a daunting amount of oil). Cook them each side to a deep tobacco colour. Remove to a paper towel to drain. Put in the next lot of aubergines, adding more oil, draining on a fresh set of paper towels. As you go along, start lining the bottom of a large gratin dish (no need to oil the dish as the aubergines will release yet more oil) with the slices, half a slice covering half of another slice, and so on. Do the same up the sides of the dish.

While you wait for each batch of aubergines to cook, chop 3 large ONIONS and 5 cloves of GARLIC. Start to sweat them in another frying pan with OLIVE OIL. Cook gently for about 40 minutes or until you have the consistency of a loose jam. Let them stick to the pan, caramelising. Turn them over, leave them to stew again, then repeat. Set aside and prepare the peppers.

When you have finished the aubergines, use the same pan, now slightly browned or burnt on the bottom, to cook 6 peppers, red, green and yellow PEPPERS, sliced lengthwise. Fry for a few minutes uncovered, then 5 or 10 minutes covered, until they wilt and burn a little. Remove and lay along the middle of the gratin dish, over the aubergine. Make a line on each side of the peppers with the onion and garlic compote.

Deglaze the frying pan with two 14oz / 400g tins TOMATOES, scraping up the browned bits from the bottom of the pan. Chop the tomatoes roughly with the side of your wooden spoon; add a pinch of instant COFFEE, SUGAR, SPICES, ORANGE PEEL and CAYENNE — ½ teaspoon of each (2 of the Cayenne if you are aiming at a dragon). Simmer at a highish bubble to reduce to half. You should have a rough purée. The tomatoes will start to stick to the pan; keep stirring, let them stick, stir again and so on, until you almost have a jam. Pour this in a ribbon around the onions in the gratin dish. Bake 10 minutes, covered, in a hot oven; then bake another 10 minutes uncovered, until caramelised. Serve with fresh BASIL and PARSLEY.

If serving cool, sprinkle 2 tablespoons of good VINEGAR onto the vegetables, tipping the gratin dish to distribute evenly. Arrange a few small Niçoise black OLIVES around the edges.

For a couscous (see page 13) I cook the vegetables together, then continue cooking them for at least 2 to 3 hours, covered for the first hour, then uncovered to thicken and caramelise into a jam almost like the above tomato purée.

Ratatouille Brûlée

This version of ratatouille is cooked to the point of almost being a jam. It needs a frame to hold it together visually and, for this, I use slices of aubergines. When cooking for eight to ten people start with two large pans. As the vegetables shrink and reduce, transfer to one.

Line a large gratin dish with the fried slices of AUBERGINE, as in the recipe Ratatouille for a dragon on page 54. In a generous quantity of OLIVE OIL, cook 3 medium ONIONS, chopped, with 4 or 5 finely chopped cloves of GARLIC. As they soften, add 3 PEPPERS, 1 of each colour, seeded and sliced; 6 small COURGETTES, unpeeled, cut in rounds; 1 AUBERGINE, peeled this time and cut in 1–2in / 2–5cm squares. Cook and stir for a few minutes, wilting the vegetables. Add a 14oz / 400g tin of Italian plum TOMATOES to each pan, with a pinch of SAF-FRON, a strip of ORANGE PEEL, ½ teaspoon each of ALL-SPICE and CUMIN; a pinch of SALT and SUGAR, a dash of CAYENNE. Cook, covered, for an hour over gentle heat.

Remove lids, cook another hour. The vegetables will start to stick. Stir occasionally, then let the bottom of the pan burn to a brown, not black, coating. Deglaze, scraping up the burning coating with a few tablespoons of water, until the bottom of the pan is once again clean. Continue to cook, stir, scrape, turning over the vegetables and distributing the burnt scrapings. This is what gives the ratatouille a special flavour. The courgette and eggplant will almost disintegrate, only the peppers will remain distinctive. Taste and adjust the seasoning. If necessary, the balance of acidity can be corrected with a dash of SALT and SUGAR, even ½ teaspoon of instant COFFEE.

Pour the ratatouille over the aubergines in the gratin dish. Sprinkle with fresh PARSLEY, BASIL and CHIVES. Warm briefly in the oven or serve later, cold, with a dash of VINEGAR – one or two tablespoons – sprinkled over the ratatouille. Tip the dish to distribute evenly.

Ladies for lunch

Elizabeth was coming to lunch. Then Debby called. 'What are you doing on Wednesday?' she asked. I told her. 'I'll join you,' Debby tells me. I loved her again, silently, for her straightforwardness and I realized this lack of protocol was a compliment only paid after many years of friendship. Something was at the back of my mind, which declared itself as Elizabeth walked in the next day. She was Debby's ex-husband's present paramour. Oh well. At least the conversation wouldn't be a revolving door on domestics and children. Other than Jonathan, they had little in common, but women are elastic creatures. Debby is as tall as most men wish to be, without her six-inch heels. She is American, brusque, positive and wonderful. Her affection is long standing. She disguises the uncertainty within her with a stride and presence that no one can ignore. Elizabeth is English, never reveals inner shadows and, somehow, leaves you undecided. She could be a Belle de Nuit, or a Belle tout court.

Along came Wednesday, as did Debby, first and prompt. I was setting the table. Salami, smoked duck, mushrooms I had steeped in cream, olive oil, garlic and lemon juice. Lavish quantities of parsley and tarragon, necessary to cut the richness and finally, slivers of onion, as thin as airmail paper. Chives would have been better, but those in the garden were poorly, under winter's mud. A salad of radicchio and romaine, tossed with walnut oil. To rinse the palate later, there were mangoes with the mint which grew under the pear tree.

Champignons Cochons

The term refers to the richness of this dish and to the nickname of the French for the English. The recipe was given to me by Chrissie, my sister-in-law. I passed it on to others, then forgot about it until it was presented back to me. It is worth resuscitating.

Wipe clean 6 large field MUSHROOMS, enough for 4 people. Slice thickly into a shallow glass or enamelled dish. Pour over the mushrooms a glass of strongly scented OLIVE OIL and a glass of single CREAM. Add 2 or 3 crushed cloves of GARLIC, the juice of a LEMON, SALT, a lot of coarsely ground PEPPER. Leave the mushrooms to absorb the cream and oil for at least 1 hour. Turn over occasionally. They absorb a surprising amount and it may be necessary to add more cream or oil, to taste.

At the last minute, toss in a truly generous quantity of PARSLEY and TARRAGON, finely chopped, as this will balance the richness of the sauce. BLACK OLIVES and a few CHIVES add the rest. The sauce is irresistible, mopped up with a fresh baguette.

The mushrooms go well with PROSCIUTTO and SALAMI – either the Italian Negroni, or if you can find it, the French Rosette.

Blend any leftovers finely and add to a simple chicken broth – almost any soup will be grateful for it.

April

... I prepared one more dinner. Opening
a can of Alpo dog food, I mixed
the contents with ...

Engaged and disengaged; elopement; a meal never to be repeated

This month, almost twenty years ago, I left my first husband, Harry, after a year and a half-old marriage. I had been introduced to Harry by an Italian-American who bore, reluctantly, the name of Teddy. Although rigidly straight, he looked more like a Capone. We had been engaged and disengaged for six years. It was summer and we were in Newport, Rhode Island. Five days after the introduction, I eloped with Harry to Maryland. We were pronounced man and wife by a judge in shirtsleeves at home, standing under a collection of toy aeroplanes, trying not to laugh at his operatic reading of the ceremony. We spent the honeymoon in a pink hotel in Bermuda, trying to cool off in its room-temperature sea.

I set up house in Harry's bachelor apartment in an area of New York called Turtle Bay which happened to be diagonally across from the apartment my grandmother had just moved to. I used to check the light in her windows at night to make sure it was not too late to call.

Harry took me to Long Island to meet his family. His mother welcomed me with wisdom in her eyes. They lived on Skunk's Misery Lane in Locust Valley. A long driveway, trees given the space and time needed to grow as wide as they were tall, and lawn, lawn, lawn; columns and portico, a graceful house that overlooked the Sound. Believing in omens, I should have noticed the consistently ominous addresses, but elopers don't stop to see. Driving there, Harry told me he came from an understated and over-established family. He was their black sheep. At the moment, he didn't work for a living. I was his fourth wife. Reliably, time explained the rest. I don't remember what we were given for dinner that evening, except for mashed potatoes and peas. Harry, having had half his stomach cut out when eighteen, preferred bland food. We went to Las Vegas a month or two later. I watched, literally, thousands of dollars roll down the drain of the craps table. Harry was thirty-two, ten years older than I, slim, tall, his thick hair grey since the age of twenty, perhaps due to the grinding pains of stomach ulcers. As he rolled the dice, his shortsighted eyes were deadpan as he invoked Lady Luck. We left the next morning, leaving behind his debts and my innocence.

In New York, we received threatening phone calls from men in black hats. Harry showed me where he kept a revolver, how to use it, just in case, then turned to the New Jersey underground betting games, and to backgammon at the Racquet Club. At eight o'clock in the evening, he would call to say he was delayed. At eleven o'clock or midnight, he walked in, shaved, and walked out again. Presumably, to a games table. Then women called. No, he wasn't in, could I take a message? They hung up. Months passed, accumulating emotional agonies. He said I was his saviour.

I prepared one more dinner. Opening a can of Alpo dog food, I mixed the contents with breadcrumbs, parsley and onion and shaped this mixture in sizzling butter, removed it and added red wine and fresh butter. Sauce marchand de vin. It was ten o'clock. He was due home, maybe. The mashed potatoes and peas were ready. He arrived, and washed down his dinner with mouthfuls of Bourbon. The smell of that drink still makes my skin react. I never told him. We divorced. I ran into him once, four years later, in a restaurant. He walked over from the bar to my table: 'Hi. I'm Harry Rumboldt, haven't we met?' I introduced myself: 'Yes. I was your wife.'

The children know all these stories. 'Alpo' is their favourite. They question me when I present them with ground meat for dinner. I tell them that cooks, like magicians, never do the same thing twice.

Hamburgers pour Canaille, Sauce Marchand de Vin

I do not recommend using dog food.

Use a good quality of ground beef, but not too lean, 1lb / 450g for two people.

Mix with your hands, 1 finely chopped medium ONION, 3 tablespoons finely chopped PARSLEY, 1 tablespoon fresh white BREADCRUMBS, 3 or 4 shakes of TABASCO, WORCESTERSHIRE SAUCE, 1 beaten EGG. Shape into thick hamburgers.

Heat a heavy pan with a little BUTTER and PEANUT OIL. Cook the hamburgers to taste, remove and keep warm. Pour off excess and burnt fat, pour in a glass of RED WINE, a little VEAL STOCK or SAUCE ESPAGNOLE if you have it. Reduce by half at high heat, scraping up the browned bits at the bottom of the pan. Thicken with 3 or 4 tablespoons of butter, whisking. Pour over the hamburgers.

Quick Sauce Espagnole: 3 or 4 LAMB AND BEEF BONES just covered with half water, half RED WINE, a shot of WHISKY; 2 chopped TOMATOES, 1 CARROT, 1 ONION, 1 stick of CELERY – all chopped; pinch ALLSPICE and GROUND FENNEL. Simmer for an hour, uncovered. Strain, simmer again until reduced by half. Add a shot of MADEIRA, taste and correct to your liking, reduce again down to a few tablespoons.

The children and I like this with POMMES SAUTÉES, on a warm plate scattered with finely sliced ONIONS. They absorb the sauce and juices from the hamburgers. Then salad on the same plate which takes on a hint of gravy.

Ground lamb is a nice change.

A rest chez Toby

I spent a weekend in Toby's cottage in Dorset. The children were not returning from their Easter holiday with Miles for another week and by then my foreign suntan would have faded. I had, once again and for the last time, disappeared for a few days, repeating the folly of January. Toby didn't comment and I didn't volunteer details, exhausted by travel and by my moth-like ability to knock myself out against light-bulbs. I could imagine Lino laughing.

In exchange for the rest and privacy, I cooked in the evenings. Saturday we had a shoulder of lamb, a piece of meat that always worries me. The proportion of fat to meat is, for me, unappealing and it is easily overcooked. I had cooked it once in America quite successfully, but I couldn't remember whether it had been rolled or left flat. Toby's oven being rather low-ceilinged, I decided to use the meat flat. I trimmed it and rubbed crushed juniper berries into the pockets and surface, with fresh peppercorns, shallots, lemon peel, raisins and cinnamon. The pepper was a little green; I had picked it off the tree two days before with delight, never having seen it grow in its natural habitat.

I roasted the shoulder at high heat for half an hour, turned off the oven and left it to finish in the remaining heat for three quarters of an hour. It was pink, which we both prefer. I had made a reduction of red wine with tomato paste and a puréed celery stalk and one carrot, which thickened as it cooked with the lamb, and slightly caramelised under the high heat.

Toby laid the table. He uses porcelain plates, all different. Some are

kept in a cupboard, some stand on a long shelf above the fireplace in the
sitting room, where we ate. We talked and then read with ease, in a
restful silence.

A Shoulder of Lamb in Dorset

I use the shoulder flat, boned. A good butcher will prepare this
properly, neatly, leaving you with just one small piece of bone at
one end, the rest to scatter around the roasting pan to give the
gravy a good, strong taste. Rolling the meat for roasting I think is
a mistake, the grain is different and proportion of fat to meat on
each slice is unappealing.

Remove any large pieces of fat from the meat, on both sides.
Lay the SHOULDER in a roasting pan large enough to hold it,
along with the bones. Rub the meat on both sides, with 3
tablespoons each of ANCHOVY PASTE and hot Dijon
MUSTARD; add the juice of a LIME, a dash of SOY, the chopped
leaves of 4 or 5 branches of fresh ROSEMARY, a dozen crushed
JUNIPER BERRIES, 2 cloves of finely chopped GARLIC, a small
glass of GIN (Gordon's has a strong juniper scent). Prick the
shoulder on both sides with a fork, distribute berries and herbs
and garlic thoroughly in and under all pockets, nooks and
crannies. Leave to marinate in a cool place or the fridge for a day
or night at least.

Roast the shoulder in its marinade, bones scattered around, at
high heat 200°C / 400°F / gas mark 6 for 30 minutes. After 15
minutes, the marinade will have caramelised. Remove, deglaze
the pan with a tablespoon of TOMATO PURÉE and MUSTARD
diluted with a glass of WHITE WINE and just a little water. Baste
the meat, return to the oven for the other 15 minutes. Cover
lightly if the top of the meat is browning too darkly. Turn off the
heat, open the oven door wide for 2 minutes, then close the door
and leave the meat to rest and finish its cooking slowly for 20 to
30 minutes. It will be pink. Carve the shoulder on the bias, as this
will produce a better balance between meat and fat.

Or, rub the shoulder and pockets with crushed JUNIPER
BERRIES, coarsely ground PEPPER, chopped SHALLOTS,
LEMON PEEL finely grated, 1/2 teaspoon each of CINNAMON

AND ALLSPICE. Scatter a small handful of RAISINS and PINE NUTS around the meat in its roasting pan, and cook at high heat as above. After the first 15 minutes, add 1 tablespoon of TOMATO PURÉE diluted with 1 tablespoon of good VINEGAR and half a bottle of RED WINE. Continue to cook in the same way.

The shoulder of lamb usually weighs approximately 3½lb / 1.5kg, boned, sufficient for 6 people.

Lino returns to Italy; olive oil for butterflies, and goodbye

Lino called. He was returning to Italy within the next ten days. This meant he was giving himself up to the Napoleonic Code and would probably be arrested the minute he crossed the border to be held until proven innocent. Scandals break out daily in Italy, laws are made and broken accordingly. What is legal one morning could be illegal in the afternoon, he explained with impatient and nervous, exaggerated humour. But Lino was confident that he would be cleared. The five-month period of an incognito life in London was becoming frustrating. My affection and admiration for him was increased with worry. He said he would be in touch. 'I'll write to you', I said. 'What's your address, what's your name Lino, your surname?' This had been a mystery until now. He told me what to put on an envelope.

We went out to dinner. Lino suffered frequent intestinal upsets which made his outward cheerfulness all the more engaging. His order, not on the menu, confirmed his state. Verdure bolliti misti. He was brought a plate neatly laid with steamed courgettes, string beans, fennel bulbs and spinach. He asked for olive oil (a balm, contrary to popular belief), which he dribbled lightly over each vegetable. It seasoned the perfectly cooked vegetables without clouding their freshness. After tasting them, I decided to do this at home. We talked about food. He told me about a dessert that lay on the restaurant's trolley, called Tira Mi Su, made of Mascarpone in between layers of Savoyard cake dampened with a liqueur, coffee and cacao. 'It is called this way because it is afrodisiaco. How would you translate?'

'Literally will do,' I said: 'Pull Me Up.'

He told me about his grandfather's household. Up until the early fifties, the six or seven peasants working on the property came once a week to the house to bake bread, not having ovens of their own. One would bring the wood, the other prepare the oven, a third would light it. Each had his role and place in the queue, alternating each week, so that they each had a turn for the first loaf out of the oven. Always white bread. Zero zero graded flour was the most prized. Only rich people indulged in poor wholewheat flour.

Lino took me home early, with courteous flourishes. As always, the sweeping glance at my street, at myself – all was clear and good. 'Ciao, pazzina.* Don't get into trouble, anything you need, call me. I am at your disposal.'

*diminutive endearment of pazza = loony.

May

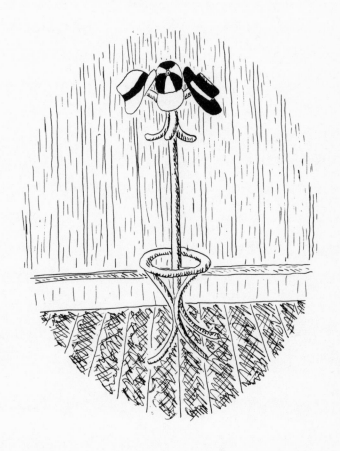

... For a few months I entered the
triangle. I saw the world and my
world from these three perspectives...

Three Musketeers come for dinner

Sitting in bed with the usual café au lait one morning, I visualized stairs, unending. One step leads to another whether you watch or not. One year ago I met Ann, an editor to whom I'd sent material. One step. We had lunch. In February, she invited me to a dinner at the Chelsea Arts Club. I met Murray. Eccentric, mischievous and like many people who are broke, generous with time and thought. Murray was a living oxymoron and painted paradoxes. I was asked to another of those dinners. I met Robert. Theoretical or was it rhetorical Robert. An academic with a white face and long limbs who smiled after sunset and listened to modern jazz. A week or two later, Robert asked me back to the club for a drink. I met Peter. Sociologically converted, uncompromising Peter, whose nefarious reputation ran past the reality of his deeds. They called themselves The Three Musketeers. But late at night they hailed each other as Straw Man, Cowardly Lion, Tin Man. There was an exclusive but fragile perimeter around their friendship. They were funny, provocative and thirsty. For a few months I entered the triangle as the fourth musketeer.

Now, the musketeers were coming to dinner. Of my friends, I invited Debby and her husband James, a solicitor. Debby walked in first, wearing skin-tight white satin trousers and a canary yellow satin blazer, left ajar, that showed a tight lime-coloured top. The musketeers were in the garden. As the glowing and superb satinned figure appeared in the doorway saying 'Hi', they stood like exclamation marks. They had earlier predicted that my friends would be 'posh', mentally and physically draped in chintz curtains. They moved slowly, one after the other, towards Debby and James. I was anxious that these worlds might collide and was counting on at least two people to make an open-minded effort, whether induced by anthropological curiosity or sympathy. It was warm and we ate outside. By the time we were half way through the bourride, spooning aïoli over the fish in its broth and opening the seventh bottle of Fitou, the noise had risen, Murray made a speech, Robert stood on his chair to reply with another, Peter and Debby were shouting flirtatiously across the table and James was counting the four letter words, wondering at the limited use of vocabulary. I was pleased. The wide sea of social difference was drunk.

These dinners continued. A week or two later, the musketeers brought Philip, a man without an address, dressed with an immaculate blazer, pink shirt, discreet gold cufflinks, navy tie, pink handkerchief in breastpocket, grey trousers with perfectly steamed front pleats. Murray wore a black and white checked suit, matching shoes and a plantation straw hat. The others came in jeans and t-shirts. Philip brought Millie. Inquisitive, talkative, circles under her eyes. Peter brought Clarissa. The bright and insecure rebel daughter of aristocrats. As a contribution she and Peter brought fresh crab, which they could not afford, and a bowl of mayonnaise made with sesame oil. It wasn't very good but the gesture and their presence gave it a nice taste. I brought up the subject of astrology, about to reveal my grandmother's clairvoyant career, but Peter walked out of the room peremptorily. He did not have the time to listen to such nonsense. I didn't have the courage to tease his prejudice.

After the crab, we had a summer stew of veal, with tomatoes, courgettes, green olives and white wine. Tasting it that afternoon, I added a little vinegar and a teaspoon of olive paste. I made Judith Olney's oven croûtons, seemingly lighter at that time of year than sautéed potatoes, but that was an illusion, as were some of my dinner guests. Towards the end of the dinner, we sang national anthems. Murray's lady being German, Philip, for reasons of his own pretending to be Australian, and myself feeling more French than American that evening, the octet was a cacophonic descant. Murray seemed to peer intently at the rest of us, through his round glasses as though through binoculars and his smile was thoughtful and observant. At the far end of the table, Robert leant lizardly back in his chair. His glasses were folded in the breastpocket of his white jacket and had the effect of a silk handkerchief. Peter, on my left, laughed loudly and often. Perhaps that was why he seemed highly charged. Or was it a trick of the candlelight?

I thought of the test of time and hallucinatory pleasure. One of the three musketeers, the happiest with himself, might remain a friend. The other two, their study accomplished, would move on.

A Summer Stew of Veal for Musketeers

This served 3 hungry musketeers and their companions. I used 3lb / 1.3kg of VEAL, cut into 1–2in / 5cm pieces. For this I buy either the loin or leg.

Slice 4 large ONIONS; cook with 4 or 5 finely chopped cloves of GARLIC in OLIVE OIL until softened. Add 3 small COURGETTES, unpeeled and sliced in rounds; a handful of

CHERRY TOMATOES, 1 small AUBERGINE, unpeeled, cut in rounds then quartered. Sweat the vegetables with the onions and garlic, adding a little more olive oil, SALT and freshly ground PEPPER. Cook for 5 minutes, add 1 tablespoon of TOMATO PURÉE, 1 tablespoon of OLIVE PASTE, diluted with 2 glasses of dryish WHITE WINE. Add a dash of CIDER or SHERRY VINEGAR, a handful of unpitted GREEN OLIVES, a few strands of SAFFRON, a slice of ORANGE PEEL. Simmer uncovered, for 45 minutes to an hour, when the vegetables and liquid thicken. Set aside.

Brown the pieces of VEAL on all sides at medium heat in OLIVE OIL. Do this in batches so that the juices of the meat can evaporate and not stew the veal instead. When finished, deglaze the pan with a little WHITE WINE, scraping up the browned solids. Return all the veal to the pan, add the vegetables, continue to cook at a medium to low heat for 10 minutes, just long enough for the veal to be moist and tender, just past the point of being pink. Serve with PARSLEY and FRESH MINT, finely chopped together, incorporated throughout the dish as well as over it – or BASIL and CHIVES.

Croûtons for Musketeers

This is a slight variation on a recipe of Judith Olney's called Pulled Bread.

Use a fresh loaf of good WHITE BREAD. Cut the crust off one end and pull out pieces of various sizes, up to 3in / 7.5cm (it will shrink during the cooking). Lay in a baking tin, pour over BUTTER melted with a little crushed GARLIC, CAYENNE and chopped CHIVES or finely chopped SPRING ONIONS. Roll the bread evenly in the melted butter. Bake in a medium hot oven until evenly browned, about 40–60 minutes. Serve sprinkled with PARSLEY.

These croûtons melt in the mouth, a delicious substitute for sautéed potatoes. It looks lighter but isn't.

A lunch in America; the fourth cat

The year Miles and I moved to Beaver Dam, we met Tony and Roxana. Their house was four miles up the road; months of Sunday evenings passed, the roots of our friendship spread further and further, beyond the span of common ground. We introduced them to our visiting friends from abroad, the most important being Ian, who in turn became as close and as fond of them as we were. Gordoni, our latinization of Ian's surname, looks more and more like Peter Finch, superimposed over Beethoven; his features improve with each year in the way that is only given to men and wine. Ian's wit can bite, but he is one of the few Englishmen I know who hugs a friend, if at all, with Latin enthusiasm.

On summer weekends we ate lunch on the deck outside the kitchen, the air noisy with katydids (as Americans call crickets) and tree frogs, the stream below. One particular lunch, I had included a local couple, a tentative exception to our prejudice towards county natives who bored us, and of course Tony and Roxana, now part of this insular family. Ian sat between Roxana and Lucy. We would be told much later, that Flucy, as Ian nicknamed her, took an immediate shine to him. There had been legwork under the table, as we ate our lapin au romarin et olives noires.

Aware that many Americans consider rabbits as pets rather than meals, I produced lunch without comment, but the mystery was not to last. Miles and Ian, over breakfast, exchanged their views on bores and looking up at me as I cleared the table, announced that Mrs Morland stood on her own as top bore of Westchester, shunned by the locals who would not include this foreign and unsporting lady in their tennis and golf parties. Mrs Morland pointed out that sports bored her. Miles and Ian expanded the theme as they supervised my preparations for lunch and decided expected guests would be tested. As we started, one asked:

'What can this boring dish be?'

'Reminds me of cat.'

'Oh yes, had a rat in Spain once, rather bland.'

I muttered lapin for culinary elegance but it did not help. I don't remember Lucy consuming much more of her meal. Tony, who has a palate for le goût du terroir, ate well and more with the rest of us.

Roxana has the sort of fine, elusive features that are affected by mood. Across the table, she seems delicate. Her height takes me by surprise as she rises to tell a story, feet and hands precisely poised for punctuation, her stance a cross between that of ballet dancer and toreador. Her stage sense and talent for mimicry are exuberant.

I went to New York recently and spent a day and an evening with Tony and Roxana in Westchester. Willow Green Farm is a full house, with three cats and two dogs. Rocky, Roxana's daughter, was curled up on the rug by the fire in the library, like a fourth cat, reading a book. Later she made a gingerbread cake for dinner which we ate hot with cream. I made an anchovy sauce for lamb chops which I thought tasted of jet lag and amorous fatigue, but as I left Roxana stood on the station platform saying the sauce was delicious and 'Oh Guislaine, I wish you would come back to us.'

Lapin au Romarin

Debby asked her butcher for a rabbit, one day in July. Being out of season, he produced one that was deep frozen.

'Will it taste of chicken?' she asked.

'Certainly not,' he assured her.

Debby had never cooked a rabbit, this one was still furry; she asked her butcher to prepare it for her. She would return the next day. A woman standing behind asked if she could have the feet, if Debby didn't mind. 'My cat loves to play with them,' she explained. Debby, beginning to have doubts, said yes, she was welcome to the feet, no longer associating them with good luck, and forgot to enquire what sort of rabbit this was. The next day, she found out it was 'domestic' but not 'bred'. Ambiguous; and she was surprised to discover that the rabbit, once prepared, would be skinless.

'Only rabbits on the Continent have skin,' the butcher said.

'I just love the English,' Debby said to me, as she told me the story.

Debby used the following recipe; the rabbit tasted of chicken. Other than that, she thought it was a good dinner. So – if you have a source of wild rabbit, place the RABBIT 3–4lb / 1.3–1.7 kg in weight and cut in 8 pieces, in a deep glass or porcelain bowl. Cover with water and a tumblerful of VINEGAR. Leave for an hour or two. Remove and dry. Don't bother with the marinade if using specially bred rabbit.

Cook 4oz / 100g diced PANCETTA (about 1in / 2.5cm thick) in a little OLIVE OIL in a large frying pan, until browned and lightly crisp. Set aside. Using the pancetta fat, and a little extra olive oil, fry the rabbit in batches, for 4 or 5 minutes on each side, until golden. Discard any burnt fat, add a little fresh olive oil. Add 2 broken BAY LEAVES and 3 tablespoons chopped, fresh ROSEMARY. Stir for a few seconds, pour in a glass of WHITE

WINE, a tablespoon of good SHERRY VINEGAR. Scrape up the solids on the bottom of the pan, stir in a tablespoon of TOMATO PASTE. Return the pancetta and the rabbit pieces, and 6–10 chopped ANCHOVY FILLETS. Cover, simmer gently for an hour, occasionally checking the level of the liquid. Adjust, if necessary, with a little more wine or STOCK. I usually add another tablespoon or two of vinegar, but you may not agree – as it cooks, the balance evens itself. At the end, squeeze in the juice of half a LEMON.

While the rabbit simmers, cook 6 red PEPPERS, sliced lengthwise, in olive oil at medium heat, until they wilt, brown and in parts, burn. Add chopped GARLIC during the last 2 or 3 minutes, SALT and freshly ground PEPPER.

Transfer the rabbit and sauce to a serving dish, surround with the peppers, garlic and anchovies. Serve with fresh PARSLEY.

Lapin aux Noix

This is my father's recipe, marked 'superbe'. It should be prepared in the autumn when fresh, milky walnuts are available. For 6 people you will need 2 wild RABBITS, if they are about 3lb / 1.3 kg in weight each.

Two wild RABBITS, each cut into eight pieces, and their livers; 6–8oz / 150–200g FRESH WALNUTS, shelled; WALNUT OIL; 2 glasses of SAUTERNES; 6 cloves of GARLIC, finely chopped; Dijon MUSTARD à l'ancienne (with seeds); 10 fl oz / 280ml of CHICKEN STOCK.

In a large pan, heat a glass of walnut oil with a little sweet BUTTER. When almost hot, put in enough rabbit pieces, uncrowded, to brown evenly on all sides. Remove to an oven-proof casserole. When all the pieces are done, pour out burnt fat, deglaze the pan with the Sauternes, add half the walnuts, lightly chopped, the stock, a broken BAY LEAF, the garlic and livers of the rabbits, roughly chopped. Stir for a minute at medium heat, stir in two tablespoons of the mustard and pour over the rabbit.

Cover and bake in a medium hot oven for 45 minutes. Let rest, heat turned off, for 10 minutes. Taste for seasoning, add freshly ground PEPPER and the rest of the walnuts. Serve with fresh PARSLEY and a few leaves of THYME.

Lamb Chops with Anchovy Sauce

This is a surprisingly good marriage, the anchovies not obvious, quickly and simply done. For four people: prepare a paste of 6 to 10 ANCHOVY FILLETS, chopped and mashed with 1 tablespoon of TOMATO PURÉE, 2 tablespoons of hot Dijon MUSTARD, a dash of SOY and TABASCO and WORCESTERSHIRE SAUCE, a shot of Gordon's GIN, 2 glasses of RED WINE. Set aside.

Using a heavy cast iron pan, fry the LAMB CHOPS at high heat so that they seal quickly on both sides, using just a little PEANUT OIL. Turn the heat down slightly, continue to cook for 2 to 3 minutes on each side, depending on the thickness of the lamb chops and how pink you like them. Remove and keep warm. Pour out excess burnt fat from the pan, deglaze with the red wine and anchovy mixture, at high heat. As it reduces to not quite half, whisk in two or three knobs of BUTTER. Pour over the lamb chops, serve sprinkled with fresh PARSLEY and coarsely ground PEPPER.

To keep warm while eating a starter – undercook the lamb chops by 3 or 4 minutes. Leave in an oven heated to a medium heat. Turn off the oven; the lamb chops will continue to cook slowly and evenly. They will wait without overcooking.

A Daughter's Hot Gingerbread

Rocky is thirteen, pretty, intricate – you don't forget her. We ate the gingerbread hot, with cream. It was sticky and delicious, lingering with the last sip of wine. Here are her instructions, unedited, sent to me a few days ago with a note from Roxana: '. . . very hot outside . . . pink lilies are a big steamy mass . . . the gardenia plant has two perfect blossoms . . . a smell that makes you close your eyes.'

½ cup soft SHORTENING (BUTTER), 2 tablespoons SUGAR, 1 EGG, 1 cup MOLASSES, 1 cup boiling water, 2¼ cups WHITE FLOUR, 1 teaspoon SODA, ½ teaspoon SALT, 1 teaspoon GINGER, 1 teaspoon CINNAMON.

Heat oven to 325°C / 170°F / gas mark 3. Grease and flour pan. Mix butter, sugar, egg. Blend in molasses and water. Then add everything else. Pour into pan. Bake 45 to 50 minutes.

Measurements are American. As long as you use the same cup throughout, proportions will fit. Flour is measured by volume, not weight. Use a small loaf-shaped tin.

A return; cooking at Willow Green Farm

I stood in line in Fratelli's Delicatessen, daydreaming. Mrs Massina's shadow crossed my unfocussed gaze, carrying a steaming platter of fried octopus. She laid the dish in her husband's shop window. The smell was disturbing. It took me back to a particular meal, to its slow making, to the pervasive smell and to the emotion that went into it.

For a week in May two years ago, Miles and I went to New York. The date coincided with Tony's birthday. A few days before, Roxana and I, from respective sides of the Atlantic, discussed the menu for his dinner party. 'How about a bourride?' I asked, knowing it to be a favourite of Tony's. 'Why don't you do it?' Roxana answered. We went over the shopping list. She confirmed that my fishmonger was still there. Three days later, Miles and I arrived in New York, on a Thursday afternoon. It seemed a miracle, the next morning, twenty-four hours later, to have crossed a continent, to be walking on American soil, down Madison Avenue on my way to Grand Central Station to catch a train to Katonah, Westchester County, where Tony and Roxana lived, as we had, with suitcases and a shopping list for dinner. With a little more concentration, I might be just going home after a long absence. My adjustment to time and distance is primitive, aeroplanes bewilder me.

Roxana met me at the station in Katonah with two baskets. We spent the next two hours turning the Atlantic telephone list into food. We were served by the same scowling figure in Conte's Fishmarket; Joe still made perfect mozzarella in the back of his delicatessen; Weinstein the chemist asked if I needed any more of my scent. I reminded him that I didn't live here any more, and I knew that I wished that I did. We returned to Willow Green Farm, Tony and Roxana's nineteenth-century, white clapboard house, with heavy baskets. We walked along the brick path to the back door and were met by the two marmalade and twin cats: Tippers, my own, left behind along with plants, and Tiger, standing under Roxana's giant black poodle. I noticed the dangling legs of hornets as they flew up in fine zigzags against the white boards of the house, the sound of grasshoppers, scratching at their unshaven legs in the long grasses up in the fields. And the heat, which felt like anxiety because I was too pleased to be back.

We unpacked the food, but not my suitcase, and had lunch. Slices of mozzarella still dripping from the brine it had been pulled out of minutes ago, threaded with olive oil, fresh pepper and basil. It was buttery and warm. We sat at the kitchen table, looking out on the garden, a Lutyens bench in the background and, above and beyond it, the paddocks. We had a little white wine and drank to the old and other days, adding this one.

I rolled up my sleeves and took over the kitchen, continuing a tradition for my father who invariably ends up cooking in other people's houses. The walls were painted in the deep blue the Italians use to keep the flies away from their own kitchens. I admired the oiled wood counters, cabinets and, in the centre, 'the piano' as the French call it, an enormous restaurant gas stove called a Vulcan, which has a respected presence. It is a deep, matte black. I tied my apron, feeling territorial. Dinner the next evening being for twelve, there was a generous quantity of food to work with. Six pounds of red snapper, halibut fillets, skin left on one side, squid, mussels; four big fish heads (split) and backbones; carrots, onions, leeks, one red pepper, new and waxy potatoes; saffron, allspice, Chinese five spices, Cayenne, mace, nutmeg, cinnamon, ground coriander, Worcestershire sauce, a slice of orange peel, tomato paste; oils and wines and home-made chicken stock.

I started the fish stock: heads and backbones covered with water, a bottle of red, and a bottle of white wine. That was to simmer for an hour, thirty minutes longer than is advised in cookbooks, for a reason unknown and unheeded by me. I used two large pots, large enough for it to be a struggle to get them over to the sink for straining. Tony walked in the door just at that moment. He relieved me of one big pot and then the other. We greeted each other over steaming fish. I returned the same two pots, now strained, to the stove, anticipating with pleasure the next and best part in the making of a bourride. All the spices were lined up and ready on the counter. I smelled them one by one and put in a generous pinch of each, sometimes two. Then the vegetables, neatly chopped by Roxana, left as a nature morte on another counter.

It was too early for anyone but the cook to taste the stock, but Tony did anyway: 'It's got a long way to go – lucky I know the cook personally.' Roxana kneaded her dough, making approving noises. I liked her loaves of brown bread, but thought they were a bit crumbly. Purposely so, she explained later, outraged and forgiving.

I prepared the squid, slicing it in rings, shortening the tentacles but leaving a part attached to the base. They would look like sea flowers once cooked. I warmed the fish in strong olive oil, a great deal of finely chopped garlic, and let this cook gently in a sauteuse until syrupy, sticky and lightly caramelised. As I write this, I can recall the smell, the cats lifting their noses, rubbing against my legs, leaving a ring of fur around my trousers. Then a ladle of stock is poured over the squid and its juices and reduced again to near-caramel. This goes on, and on, for an hour or more (the precision of my timing is a little Latin). You add a large tin of Italian plum tomatoes (fishing out the rather sad basil leaf put in for useless effect) and a dozen or so of the new potatoes. That bubbles and reduces along with the red pepper cut into indiscreet pieces so that they may be found later and blended into the rouille that accompanies the meal. The fiddling with the stock continues and the squid is set aside. I taste, smell, walk away and then return a moment later for another sniff (the nose gets tired and becomes a less reliable instrument), taste again and add more of everything, but only the one piece of orange peel. Its potency, relative to size, is surprising. By six that evening, the stock was down to one pot (strained of vegetables after two hours, which sometimes I blend into a fine purée and put back into the pot for thickening, but not this time, for the good reason that Roxana couldn't find her machine) and developing character. It needed something more. I went into Tony's drink cupboard to take a small glass of whisky and one of dry vermouth, then poured both in. Now it smelled right. The colour had changed from a watery grey to a pale copper, to a warmer tint of reddish brown earth. Tony tasted it again. The skeleton of the soup was there. We left it on a very low flame to grow the rest of its body. I went upstairs to unpack and change.

I came down just as Miles arrived from town. The reunion was complete. After a drink we sat down to dinner, once more at the kitchen table, now candlelit. The table was up against the window. We were multiplied by our reflections, under the green, opaque glass shade of a pool table light. It made an intimate circle of illumination down over the plates. Roxana brought us a sizzling gratin dish of pork chops, grilled in olive oil and scented with crushed juniper berries, fennel seeds, lemon and garlic, a meal I had roughly adapted from Elizabeth David and passed on. A different personality each time, and good. Across the kitchen, the bourride simmered, gaining independence, while Roxana and Miles happily argued about the American writer Norman Mailer, a habit they acquired years ago.

On our way to bed, we laid the bourride to rest in the cool back entrance, amongst boots, hats, coats and away from the inquisitive animals of the house. Roxana patted me on the shoulders. I patted the pot. Pungent smells followed us upstairs.

The next morning, I awoke early and went for a walk with my cat, out the back door, past the bourride and into the familiar woods and pasture, noticing what I used to take for granted. The heat still made me anxious.

After breakfast, I made the rouille: an aïoli I make with a handful of bread, soaked in the fish stock and made complex with the finely puréed red pepper and Cayenne; later, I returned the bourride (now deserving its name) to a small flame and added the squid with its pungent reduction. The rest of the day was free. I wrapped Tony's presents: a whistling mug from me and a bottle of Château Margaux, the vintage being that of his birthday, from Miles.

Three minutes before dinner, precisely this time, as the fish must not be overcooked and it goes on cooking at table in the heat of the soup, I put in the mussels and the fish fillets cut into fork-sized pieces. At the last minute, lots of parsley; no herbs as they would argue with so many spices, although I do throw in three or four bouquets garnis during the stock's build up. There were croûtons for each, left in a slow oven for an hour and a half to absorb oil and butter at a slow pace. The table was laid in the dining room, everything was ready.

After the bourride there were cheeses, a salad of watercress, endives and buttercrunch lettuce, then a chocolate cake made without flour or sugar, brought by one of the guests. It was excellent but I thought a little heavy on the tongue after bourride. Memory of people and conversation is hazy. My focus was inward, I concentrated on food, skirting the overwhelming feeling of being happy for the wrong reasons. I remember Miles leaving the table early but returning a little later in his dressing gown and some of us were in the middle of arguing about the merits of hugging, the Anglo-Saxon reluctance towards physical manifestations of affection. I think we went to bed at three in the morning. A successful evening, or so everyone said.

There went Friday and Saturday. Sunday was idle. We walked the grounds of our old house feeling anti-clockwise.

Monday, Miles returned to London and I went in to New York City to stay with other friends for three more days. The last morning, I took my breakfast to the window and pulled up a chair, resting my feet on the ledge – beyond them a view of brownstones and roofs and water tanks and chimneys, a tree, skyscrapers. Windows and a glimpse of a room's interior. Heat came at me through the window; the sound of cars on warm tar; air-conditioners and radios. I was to return the next day to London. Home?

Willow Green Farm Pork Chops with Juniper

This is Roxana's recipe, an interpretation of mine which is an interpretation of a recipe of Elizabeth David's. Cooking is a game of Chinese whispers and whispers get better the more they travel. The following will feed four people.

Use PORK CHOPS at least 1in / 2.5cm thick. Marinate overnight or at least several hours, in an enamelled gratin dish, with 2 tablespoons of crushed JUNIPER BERRIES, 6 table-spoons of OLIVE OIL, the juice of a LIME, 2 teaspoons FENNEL SEEDS lightly crushed with a tablespoon of PEPPERCORNS. Once in a while, prick the meat and turn over.

Remove the dish, if it has been refrigerated, for at least an hour before cooking, so that the meat reaches room temperature. Prepare a mixture of 1 heaped tablespoon of strong Dijon MUSTARD diluted with a shot of Gordon's GIN (strong juniper scent), a dash of TABASCO and WORCESTERSHIRE SAUCE.

Place the chops, with marinade, under a hot grill. Brown well for 10 minutes. Add the mustard mixture, turn over the chops, grill for another 10 to 15 minutes. Let rest in a just-warm oven for 5 minutes. Serve with fresh PARSLEY. There will only be a spoonful or two of sauce but its essence is strong and will have permeated the meat.

Or, if your grill collapses as mine just did: brush off the marinade from the pork chops. Heat a heavy cast-iron pan, with 3 tablespoons OLIVE OIL. As it almost starts to smoke, put in the pork chops. Cook three minutes on each side at high heat so that they are almost charred. Pour off the burnt fat, add a tablespoon of fresh oil and the marinade, the mustard mixture, a glass of WHITE WINE. Cover, simmer over a gentle heat for 15 minutes. Leave to rest for 5 minutes.

Une Bourride

I have watched my father prepare a bourride many times; I take my system of 'stream of consciousness' from him. The spices and wines used vary according to time, place and temper. This recipe is a rough guide, for twelve people. It is quite long and preparing the *stock* a day or two ahead of time helps. I allow 8oz / 225g of fish per person and depending on where you are, I suggest any of the following or a combination of several: HALIBUT, TURBOT, MULLET, MONKFISH, SWORDFISH, BASS, KINGFISH, SCALLOPS, SQUID, MUSSELS (if small and fresh). The fish should be filleted, skin left on one side so that it doesn't fall apart in the soup.

The *croûtons* are made of stale WHITE BREAD, 1 slice per person, crust removed, laid in a baking tin and brushed with melted BUTTER mixed with PARSLEY, left in a low oven for about 1½ hours, turning them over once. Time is flexible, leaving you free to concentrate during the last hour, on the bourride.

The stock: Use at least 4 large FISH HEADS and BACKBONES, each weighing between 1–2lb / 450–900g, rinsed and, if available, SHELLS from LOBSTER, CRAB and SHRIMP. Cover with cold water, 1 bottle of RED WINE, 1 bottle of WHITE WINE. Bring to a slow boil, skim the froth as it rises. Add 2 tablespoons of good VINEGAR; simmer for 45 minutes to an hour, depending on its taste. Strain, return broth to another clean stockpot.

Add chopped vegetables: 2 LEEKS, 2 ONIONS, 2 CARROTS, 2 sticks of CELERY or FENNEL BULBS; a generous pinch of SAFFRON, 1 level teaspoon each of ALLSPICE, CAYENNE, CHINESE FIVE SPICES, MACE, NUTMEG, CINNAMON, crushed CORIANDER SEEDS, ground CUMIN; several shakes of WORCESTERSHIRE SAUCE; a strip of ORANGE PEEL, 1 pint / 550ml of CHICKEN STOCK, two 14oz / 400g tins of Italian PLUM TOMATOES. Simmer gently for 2 hours. Strain. If you wish a slightly thick soup, purée 2 ladles of the vegetables in a blender and return to the soup.

Store for a day or two, or continue: if using SQUID, cut the tentacles almost up to the body, leaving 1in / 2.5cm or so. Once cooked, the body will curl into a sea flower-like shape. Warm the squid pieces in strong OLIVE OIL, a good deal of CHOPPED GARLIC, and cook gently for an hour. As it starts to stick and caramelise during this hour, add a ladle of warm stock. Reduce until almost dry, add another ladle of stock and so on. With the last ladle of stock, add 1 sweet RED PEPPER, roughly cut. Cook until the pepper wilts. Remove the red pepper pieces and blend to a fine consistency with a little of the soup. Reserve the squid and puréed pepper in separate bowls.

Continue to simmer the soup which, by now, should be turning a good red earth colour. After tasting, add a glass of WHISKY and a glass of dry VERMOUTH, a few more spices if it seems a little undefined. Simmer another hour. Transfer to the final pot. As you do this, check the quantity. I allow 4 ladles per person. If there is too much, freeze the extra for another use or reduce a little longer. If you are a little short, add more RED WINE and CHICKEN STOCK.

Add the squid and 2 or 3 potatoes per person, preferably small new ones. Keep at a barely perceptible simmer and make the *rouille*. Into a copper or earthenware bowl narrowing at the bottom, pour a little STOCK onto a slice of WHITE BREAD, crust removed. Crumble and mix. Add 8 crushed cloves of GARLIC, the puréed RED PEPPER and a good pinch of CAYENNE or a little spoonful of HARISSA (see page 13). It should be quite hot. Whisk and combine well. Add 4 EGG YOLKS. Slowly whisk in 1–1½ pints / 550–850ml of olive oil. As it thickens, add a squeeze of LEMON JUICE, then a tablespoon of warm water. Continue to add the olive oil. Check the seasoning and set aside. Do not refrigerate. The occasional addition of warm water allows more oil to be absorbed into the emulsion and prevents an oily film rising to the top of the rouille.

Have the fish ready, cut into manageable pieces, also the mussels and scallops. When ready to serve, add the fish to the bourride, simmer very gently for three minutes. Add the mussels and scallops. After one minute bring to the table where fish and shellfish will finish cooking. Sprinkle with PARSLEY. Place a few croûtons in each bowl, the bourride over that, then a generous spoonful of the *rouille*.

June

... "Hooligan, coll., U. S.,"
spoke the sociological dictionary.

Lino is arrested; Musketeers return for more; a cassoulet

Heard from Giovanna that Lino was arrested the instant he crossed the Italian border. He spent ten days in prison, or al collegio, as he put it. He had now been released, but was to remain in his apartment for one month. His passport was confiscated. He was not allowed to leave the premises of his home. Compared with the cell that measured eighteen square metres and held nine men, his apartment would be immense and fresh. Giovanna expected that by July he would be free to move within the city, if not join her on a seaside holiday.

She had called me late in the afternoon. I was preparing another Musketeer dinner. This time, a cassoulet. Never mind the wrong time of year. They wanted more of my food, they said, one of them pointing out it was cold enough for baked beans. I thought of Belloc's lion: 'When first your toes and then your heels, and then by gradual degrees . . .'

I sifted the flageolets through my fingers, rejecting the occasional grit and pebble, and put them into a stock of chicken, white wine, allspice, saffron and Chinese Five Spices. I had bought a few pieces of confit d'oie and two saucissons de Toulouse from my French butcher in Pimlico. I put the latter into a shallow pan and simmered them for twenty minutes in red wine and a little water. Later, I would reduce this liquor and add it to the cassoulet.

The three men arrived, discussing social category. Murray looked at me: 'This one is easy – no category, therefore no class.' His eyes were upside down with delight. 'Hooligan, coll., U.S.,' spoke Robert, the sociological dictionary. Peter followed me into the kitchen to inspect the cassoulet. He liked food, he liked cooking. I found this reassuring, like people who understand cats.

The liquid, by now quite syrupy, was bubbling at the sides and the breadcrumbs at the top were just moist enough to brown and form a slight crust. We sat down. We spoke of houses. This one would be on the market in a few weeks' time. We drank to that, and to the next one, wherever and whatever that might be.

Cassoulet in June

In England, that year, this was appropriate. This will feed 8 to 10 people.

Spread 1lb / 450g of French FLAGEOLETS on the kitchen counter or run through your fingers to eliminate pebbles and grit. Rinse under cold water four or five times. In a large pot, cover the beans with cold water. Bring slowly to a boil, taking at least 40 minutes. As it reaches the boil, remove from heat, leave for 40 minutes. Drain outside: plants will like it, it will prevent sink and house smelling for hours unpleasantly and this first cooking removes toxins that cause indigestion.

Return to the stove, cover once more with cold water and CHICKEN STOCK, about double the volume of beans. Add one 14oz / 400g tin of Italian plum TOMATOES, 1 tablespoon TOMATO PURÉE, 2 glasses fruity WHITE WINE, 4 or 5 finely chopped GARLIC cloves, 2 chopped ONIONS, 1 chopped CARROT, 2 broken BAY LEAVES, 2 BOUQUET GARNIS; 1 level teaspoon each of ALLSPICE and CINNAMON; thick pieces of PANCETTA or a good SMOKED BACON (about 8oz / 225g), diced; a CALF'S FOOT or PIG'S TROTTER, previously blanched. Do not salt the stew. Simmer, covered, for an hour.

Prick 2 SAUCISSONS DE TOULOUSE and place, whole, in the bean pot. Cover, simmer another 15 minutes. If you can find truly good German FRANKFURTERS, put in 3 or 4, halved lengthwise. Simmer another 5 minutes.

While the beans are cooking, brown 6 LAMB STEAKS, cut from the leg; 2 PORK FILLETS, cut into thick rounds. I do not use the more traditional cuts of meat, such as shoulder – I recoil from fatty meats in stews.

Remove the Frankfurters and saucissons from the beanpot. Discard the bouquets garnis. With a slotted spoon, transfer a layer of beans into the bottom of a heavy, oven-proof, casserole or earthenware pot. Cover the beans with a layer of the saucissons, sliced thickly on the bias; a few of the browned lamb and pork pieces, then one or two halved Frankfurters. Layer with more beans. Continue to alternate, finishing with beans at the top.

Taste the remaining liquid from the beans, correct if necessary to your taste. A little more wine, tomato paste, Cayenne or pepper? Ladle enough of the liquid into the casserole to not quite cover the beans. Reserve leftover liquid. Cover the casserole and store for 24 hours in a cool place. Excess fat will coagulate at the top. Remove if there is a lot, but leave a few tablespoonfuls.

When ready, bake uncovered, in a low to medium oven, for 1 hour. Check that the beans are moist but not swimming in stock. Adjust level with reserved liquid. At the end of the hour, sprinkle with fresh white BREADCRUMBS, dribble a little reserved liquid over them, dot with BUTTER or GOOSE FAT. Bake another hour, adding half way through more breadcrumbs, stirring lightly and breaking up the first batch. Do this once more. The stock from the cassoulet should be just sufficient to bubble at the sides, dampening the breadcrumbs and forming a good crust. Serve with freshly chopped PARSLEY.

If you are able to find a few pieces of CONFIT D'OIE, add these during the last hour.

Chicken Scented with Ham

This is a recipe, once again, inspired by Elizabeth David. It is a favourite, always a success and particularly suits a cold day in winter. My version, slightly different, is for four.

Use a heavy cast-iron pot, or enamelled casserole, with tight fitting lid, just large enough to hold a 3½–4lb / 1.5–1.8kg roasting CHICKEN. If the pot is much bigger, the juices from the bird dissipate and lose their essence.

Put in the bottom of the pot 2 BAY LEAVES, crushed; 1 tablespoon FENNEL SEEDS, lightly pounded in a mortar and pestle; ½ teaspoon CHINESE FIVE SPICES. Stuff the chicken with 4 peeled GARLIC CLOVES, a strip of LEMON PEEL, a handful of CHOPPED HAM, 2 or 3 tablespoons of a MUSHROOM DUXELLE. Place the chicken on its side, over the spices, and scatter around it 12 PEPPERCORNS and 3 tablespoons of BUTTER in pieces.

Cover the pot, bake in a medium hot oven for 30 minutes. Baste the chicken, turn it over to the other side, return covered to the oven, bake for another 30 minutes. Take the pot out of the oven once again, turn the chicken breast up, baste with the juices. Return to the oven, uncovered, leave to brown another 15 minutes.

Transfer the pot to the top of the stove, on gentle heat. Fill a ladle with BRANDY, warm it over the flame and light it. Pour the flaming brandy over the chicken, simmer for a minute or two. Carve the chicken, place on a serving dish, with bits of ham and mushroom and garlic scattered around the meat. Serve the sauce separately. There won't be very much, but its essence is strong; 2 tablespoons over each portion are a delicate treat.

I resisted, the first time, the idea of using brandy, associating it with cool headwaiters catering to ces touristes, but it does indeed make the sauce perfect.

The ham I used in America came from Vermont; sweet and smoky. I haven't found a reliable equivalent here so far. Instead, I buy a thick slice of French Pyrenees ham and chop it up at home.

Quick mushroom duxelles: place as many large field mushrooms as you like on an ungreased baking tin. Bake at medium heat, stalks removed, cup side up, for 30 minutes to an hour, until they have lost all their moisture and have shrunk. Chop finely or mince in the Magimix. It will keep well in the fridge for a week; a useful addition to soups and sauces. This strengthens and concentrates the taste of the mushrooms.

A weekend in Yorkshire; curdling the mayonnaise; an education

Robert took me to Yorkshire in his white Alfa Romeo which I couldn't reconcile with the rubber-soled, lace-up shoes he wore. I had never been to this part of England and was struck by the white light, grey boulders that looked like sheep lying down, and the precise outlines of landscape as though cut with scissors. Swallows flew in little clouds like insects. We walked through Grass Wood, over old settlements, a hollow sound underfoot as though there was someone's room beneath, past the prickly branches and sweet scent of hawthorn and wild orchids. Angry seasons and a prevalent wind were imprinted on the shape of growth. Rabbit population was explosive, they scattered ahead of us like leaves. Startled, one ran straight into the flank of a lying down sheep, punched into like a duvet. We stopped and fell asleep in the sun.

Robert suggested we visit a friend who lived an hour away, isolated, but guarded by a giant frog-shaped boulder known to locals as The Prince. Harry seemed to move unencumbered by the weight of living and greeted Robert with amused affection. His house was dishevelled and welcoming. It made me think of Harry Lauder's Walking Stick, the hazel shrub that grows in a shape of wandering corkscrews. We stayed for lunch and Harry asked me to make a mayonnaise. I showed off and said of course I would, although I had to do so with a fork since he lived without gadgets, heat, hot water, let alone a whisk. The mayonnaise curdled. I began all over again, blushing. Slowly I integrated two fresh egg yolks into the curdled mess. This worked. We ate the mayonnaise with a haphazard mixture of leftover lamb and chicken, tomatoes, spring onions, strong cheese, rough bread.

Later, back in London, I stood in my kitchen wondering what to produce quickly and quietly. Robert, eloquent on the freedom of women, noted prolonged time working with pots and pans as wasted. I brought down the salami hooked up by the window and looked out. I could just see his legs and feet on the grass, motionless. Typewritten pages and my cat lay beside him. I peeled an avocado, cut it and mixed it with endives and a yellow pepper that sat in the middle of the fruit basket amongst plums and grapes. I made a dressing thick with parsley. I had a few dolmas. With the salami, all this made a nice hors d'oeuvres. I put together a quick chowder, with the leftovers of Haddock Monte Carlo (see page 90). Diluting the smoky-tasting cream with milk, I added corn, a few more tomatoes and a handful of diced potatoes. Some chicken stock. This would do.

Robert came in talking nonsense, ruffling and pulling his hair over his forehead as he spoke. Funny and cosy, the last a word he would dislike. Frightening too, as the gift of rhetoric sometimes is, but not today. We talked of philosophy, then structuralism, deconstruction – concepts that eluded me more each time he explained them. He ate, gently teasing my persistence and philosophical thirst. I ate, remarking on his appetite.

A few weeks ago, I asked him to dinner with Tony and Roxana who were staying at the house. I celebrated with fresh foie gras, sliced and lightly sautéed, washed down with Sauternes. The meal ended with freshly made chocolate truffles and more Sauternes. Robert refrained from being polemical, ate well and entertained me with amusing stories that would make me laugh. But he left early.

Mayonnaise and Relatives

Variations are endless, here are a few, starting with the basic emulsion. A copper bowl is best, otherwise a solid earthenware bowl, top diameter wider than bottom diameter. Eggs and oil should be at room temperature. In order of preference, use a wooden spoon, a whisk, a fork or hand beater. Perhaps an electric beater, but not the blender or Magimix. Speed of hand is preferable to that of electrically fuelled gadgets which tend to make the mayonnaise gluey from lack of air.

Quantity of oil will vary according to your method and to the quantity of eggs, but the following should be sufficient for 4 to 6 people.

Mix 2 EGG YOLKS with 1–3 crushed GARLIC CLOVES, depending on your taste, and a small pinch of SALT; add a dribble of OLIVE OIL, no more than 1 tablespoon, beating with a wooden spoon or whisk or fork, rapidly (there is a theory that you should not turn anti-clockwise). As the emulsion takes, beat in 2 tablespoons of the oil, in a dribble, then a tablespoon of warm water. Continue to dribble the oil, a little more, about 1 pint / 600ml in all. As the emulsion solidifies, add a few drops of LEMON JUICE and again, as it thickens more, another table-spoon of warm water. Whichever oil you choose, its taste intensifies in a mayonnaise so, for once, don't use a very green or strong olive oil. The addition of warm water will prevent an oil film settling over the mayonnaise after it rests. The water also allows more oil to be absorbed. Keep the mayonnaise in a cool place, but don't refrigerate it. I sometimes vary the oils – a light olive oil, then half way through, finish with a good peanut oil, or walnut or hazelnut oils. A dash of almond oil is another delicious variation.

Aïoli   Add at least 4 cloves of garlic to the above quantities, with a small slice of WHITE BREAD, crust removed, soaked then squeezed almost dry of either MILK or STOCK. Then proceed with the oil as above.

Rouille   Soak the bread in FISH STOCK, add a good pinch of SAFFRON and instead of warm water use a puréed red CHILLI PEPPER. It should be fiery.

Any leftover mayonnaise or aïoli is useful. Add a tablespoonful to a soup or salad dressing; or, a handful of watercress finely puréed in the blender with a little stock and rouille will make a new sauce for cold fish; or have on a picnic with hard-boiled eggs and tomatoes.

Haddock Monte Carlo

All know this dish and yet I cannot find a reference to it in any of my cookbooks. I thought I had too many, but I must be wrong. I would be curious to know the liaison with Monte Carlo, where I imagine it would be difficult to find – perhaps this haddock dish is named after the colour of Monte Carlo's flag? This is my version, and its aftermath.

Place fillets of SMOKED HADDOCK, preferably from the belly, skin side down, in a buttered, enamelled baking dish. Sprinkle on and around the fish, a few chopped TOMATOES, or halved cherry tomatoes, quartered FIELD MUSHROOMS, finely chopped SPRING ONIONS. Pour SINGLE CREAM, to not quite cover the fish, and a dribble of OLIVE OIL or a few knobs of BUTTER, depending on your inclination that day. Add coarsely ground PEPPER. Lay pieces of streaky, SMOKED BACON over the fish. Bake at moderately high heat for 25 minutes, uncovered. Occasionally spoon a little cream over the fish and vegetables, basting. Serve generously sprinkled with chopped fresh PARSLEY.

Leftovers: if the sauce has not been completely mopped up with warm crusty bread, as is usually the case, turn the rest into a *haddock chowder*. Dice a few POTATOES, 1 or 2 small ones per person, and simmer, just covered with CHICKEN STOCK. Add a handful of CORN during the last 2 minutes. Mix in the leftovers of the haddock, shredding the fish gently, then the tomatoes and mushrooms, diced, and what is left of the smoky-tasting sauce. Warm gently, adding a little MILK to your taste and fresh CHIVES.

July

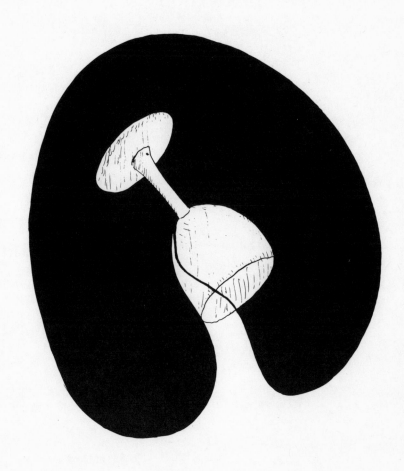

... When Murray said he was
hot and thirsty, I poured my glass
of red wine over his head ...

Summer visitors

Branko came to dinner, bringing the manuscript of his book on the therapeutic effect of humour on almost anything. His Slavic features were creased with amusement and sympathy for all, as always. I heard from Giovanna – she was renting a house on Ibiza – I might spend a week in August with her – Lino was now free, but only within Italy's borders. He would not be able to join us. Laura came to stay, from Westchester, New York. She brought her girls, who were Georgia and Tasha's best friends from the days we lived in Katonah. My father appeared out of the blue, of course, and we made a pâté de campagne, joined by the children. Counters were littered with jars of spices, bottles of wine, brandy, Madeira, oil, ground meats and chopped chicken livers, eggs, bread soaked in milk and stock, bacon and bay leaves. The mess was indescribable and effective. Five days later, we would turn out the pâté from its terrine. There was no question that it would be good.

It took a certain time to clear up the kitchen and my father suggested we might like to be taken out to dinner. He took us to a restaurant in the West End he had haunted during war days and where he used to take my mother when he was on leave. As we walked in, a pianist played Fats Waller's tune 'Your Feets Too Big'. I grew up with the sound of Fats in the background, like a family anthem. And then Gay came to stay. She is one of my younger sisters. Gay lives up to the original meaning of her name. She is not as tall as she would like to be, but the light flutter of her movements stretches her somehow. The children and I fetched her from Heathrow. She rushed towards us like a ballet dancer, feet pointing respectively at 11 o'clock and 2 o'clock, and of course, fluttering. As our cousins have said to her, her footprints are unique, she could walk barefoot in the sand and we would all be able to find her wherever she was. We hadn't seen each other in almost three years, but she was tired from her long travel from New York and quite soon after dinner we went to bed. And then kept appearing in each other's bedroom doorway to add a p.s. After the fourth appearance, we abandoned rest and sat up all night, talking, sipping iced tea with rosewater. There are six of us, from where I stand in the family, which means two brothers and four sisters, some technically half to the others, but in my mind we are a whole, if jumbled, mess of a family. The next evening, we had a dinner of roast chicken in a gravy of anchovies, vinegar and tarragon. The children brought dessert to the table. Summer pudding, made with a secret I stole from Diana, a friend in Buckinghamshire.

Iced Tea with Rosewater

This is refreshing on a hot and humid day; the taste is flowery and cleansing.

Brew 2 pots of strong TEA, using scented varieties such as Earl Grey, Lapsang Souchong, Jasmine. Strain into a large earthenware jug. Squeeze the juice of 1 ORANGE and 1 LEMON. Pour into the tea, with strips of peel. Add 3 tablespoons of SUGAR, 6 tablespoons ROSEWATER, a dozen crushed MINT LEAVES. Leave to cool and steep for at least 2 hours before drinking. If you like the taste of rosewater as much as I do, add a tablespoon to each glass you drink.

Pâté de la Maisoneuve

This is a rough country pâté, more seasoned than those distributed commercially. I don't understand the fuss or the price – it takes no more than half an hour to prepare, none of the ingredients is extravagant. This is a rough guideline – you can use a slice or two of leftover game instead of the smoked ham; a layer of spinach, briefly blanched and squeezed dry, a scattering of pitted green olives throughout. The proportion of ground meats is really up to your preference. I couldn't find pork livers last time I made this pâté; I bought instead a piece of boudin from my French butcher, about 4in/10cm long.

For ten to twelve people you will need 8oz / 225g each of: lean PORK, VEAL, LAMB, SAUSAGE MEAT (spicy), CHICKEN LIVERS, the paler the better, green shadows removed and PORK LIVERS, coarsely ground; 1in / 2.5cm thick slice of SMOKED HAM or JAMBON DE BAYONNE; 1 slice WHITE BREAD, crust removed; a reduction of MADEIRA, MARSALA, BOURBON, RED WINE, VINEGAR, JUNIPER BERRIES, BAY LEAF; 1 small EGG, beaten; 12 strips of BACON; 2 tablespoons dry GREEN PEPPERCORNS; CORIANDER and FENNEL SEEDS; ALLSPICE, FENNEL, NUTMEG, SALTPETRE, PEPPER, BAY LEAVES, SALT; 3 cloves GARLIC, finely chopped.

Reduce to 5 fl oz / 150ml half a bottle of red wine with a shot each of marsala or port, Madeira, bourbon, a tablespoon good sherry vinegar, with a dozen crushed juniper berries and a broken bay leaf. Let cool. Leave the chicken livers to marinate in this reduction for an hour or two. Leave the pork livers to soak in a little MILK alongside.

Dry and chop the chicken livers coarsely, reserving the marinade. Dry the pork livers and grind roughly in the Magimix or chop finely with a knife.

Mix the ground meats with the spices, saltpetre, coriander and fennel seeds quickly toasted in a drop of OIL, and garlic. I use a good ½ teaspoon of the nutmeg, a whole teaspoon of the other spices, sometimes exchanging cumin for fennel. Add the slice of bread, soaked and well squeezed from the marinade, the beaten egg. Mix in the pork livers. I use my hands; more gentle.

Line a terrine, bottom and sides, with the strips of bacon overhanging the edges of the terrine. Good quality fresh bacon, or sweetly smoked, whichever is the best you can find and feel like. If you use the smoked bacon, don't add salt to your mixture. Place two or three bay leaves or sprigs of THYME on the bottom in a nice pattern (this will be the top when you decant the pâté). Over the bay leaves put half the mixture of ground meats. Cover with a layer of the chicken livers and a slice of smoked ham. Pack down, cover with the rest of ground meats. Tap the terrine dish hard on the counter a few times to settle pockets of air. Fold the overhanging slices of bacon over the top, overlapping; cover tightly with foil and lid. Place in a pan of hot water and bake in a medium to low oven for 2 to 3 hours. Test that juices are slightly pink. Since you are using pork the inner temperature should be at a minimum of 160°F / 70°C.

Remove from the oven and the pan of water. Cool. Put onto a large dish, uncover and place a plate on top and weigh down, catching the juices that will spill over onto the dish. (They will cool into a gelée for later, or can be used for gravies.) I use tins of food, weighing up to 2lb / 900g, on the plate. Heavier than that compresses the pâté too much. Refrigerate for at least 3 days, but remove the weights after a few hours.

To decant, loosen the edges several times, sit in hot water for a few minutes, turn upside down onto a serving dish. This can take many energetic shakes – the suction is strong. Remove the strips of bacon carefully, revealing the bay leaves in a pattern, or sprigs of thyme. Surround with Niçoise black OLIVES, SPRING ONIONS, PARSLEY, CHERRY TOMATOES, a little gelée, whatever catches your fancy.

Leftovers are delicious crumbled over rice dishes such as risotto, or mixed into a thick bean and tomato stew, such as Cannellini Arrabbiata (see page 19).

Diana's Pudding

I know a lovely house in Buckinghamshire where the cook is Spanish. The children disappear like cats up trees and behind bushes, chased by the three sons of the house. I wake up peacefully on the top floor, with nothing to do but look out at the ancient arms of the oak tree outside the window. Sundays, the table is laid for a combination of at least twelve adults and children, food is independent of fashion or trend, you help yourself three times. In particular, to the summer pudding, for which Diana is famous. The second or third time we had this, still not able to work out the tiny difference that made all the difference, I asked Linda, the aide-de-camp in the kitchen, for the house secret. Just fruit and sugar, she said. I insisted. What kind of sugar. Brown? No, no, white. Do you cook the fruit in the sugar? No, she said, first cook the fruit, then put in the caramel. *Caramel?* A simple secret.

   Allowing for variety and ripeness of fruit, use about 6 oz / 150g of sugar to 2lb / 900g of fruit. RASPBERRIES, BLACK and RED CURRANTS, or, once in a very blue moon, FRAISES DES BOIS with BLUEBERRIES. Melt the sugar slowly in a heavy saucepan. As it turns to a deep tobacco colour, add two drops of mild VINEGAR to stop the caramel burning. Pour over the fruit in a deep saucepan, with half a teaspoon CINNAMON and a strip of LEMON PEEL. Cover, bring to a simmer, remove after 2 minutes. Taste and adjust to your liking. I sometimes add ROSEWATER. Leave overnight.

Line a pudding basin as usual, with ½in / 1.25cm thick slices of day-old bread, crust removed. With a slotted spoon, place the fruit in the bowl. Halfway up, add one layer of bread, put in the rest of the fruit, cover with the rest of the bread, filling any and all gaps with strips cut to size. Pour a ladle or two of the caramelised juices over the top, weigh down with a plate and weights. Refrigerate for at least one day.

Loosen the edges; decant by turning upside down onto a large serving plate. If there are any sections of bread not properly impregnated or coloured by the juices, pour a little more of the reserved juices. Heat in a small saucepan 2 or 3 glasses of the best CRÈME DE CASSIS you can find, with the rest of the reserved juice and simmer for a few minutes. Taste. Cool and serve separately, with a jug of thick cream.

Happy Birthday Musketeers

Robert's birthday was coming up, as was mine. The three musketeers organised a party at a club with jazz, and then another at my house to which they would bring food and wine. The nights blurred into one. When Murray, by now my favourite Musketeer, said he was hot and thirsty, I poured my glass of red wine over his head. He seemed to appreciate this and gave me a painting of a heart in a wine glass. His present to Robert was a watercolour of a beheaded man in a grey suit, with a pink heart shining below the waist; and mine was a print of Murray's, entitled Stardust. Then I decided to take the whole lot of them out to dinner, at my favourite French bistro. I bribed the waiters into singing La Marseillaise as they brought us coffee. By the end of the week, I was broke and ready for a holiday.

August

... I read her stories... skipping the
battles, in the shade, on a bleached
deck chair...

Summers in Andraitx; gambas and cigarettes

My mother and I used to spend long, dry summers in Andraitx, before electricity reached that tiny puerto in Mallorca. In the evenings, we sat on the terrace of Juan's Café, our postal address, always in time to watch the fishing boats enter the harbour, and see the nets, filled with luxurious piles of fish and contraband cigarettes thrown onto the jetty. The thumping sound of the engines crept under the skin, like the cicadas that gave heat a sound. We watched the paseo, picking out favourite faces and shapes, and ate Juan's charred gambas and mayonnaise which he brought us with a sentence that invariably began with francamente. The almond oil Juan used gave the mayonnaise a distinctive taste I try to, but cannot quite reproduce. And mantecados with coffee, an almond biscuit that had the texture of talcum powder, as did the dust we walked on in the streets. A few yards away stood the churros man by his machine which looked like a compressed steam engine and organ grinder. The vastly greasy smell of this Spanish doughnut curled past our nostrils like cigarette smoke. I was nine or ten the first time we went to Andraitx, and my first memories of food and smell start there. There is almond oil on my mother's skin in the sun, mixed with the sound of her friends, appearing and disappearing, in a lazy way without goodbyes. My favourite was Ali. Handsome, funny, with a voice unlike anyone else's. It could only be Ali making that noise on the station platform, or calling in the street from behind us. I would sit on our terrace in the afternoon, cooking the shrimp I had caught in a coffee strainer, by the rocks of the lighthouse. I built a small fire with parasol pine needles, and their cones. Tadé, the Polish painter with Gauloises stains on his wide fingers and crooked teeth, dropped in. Then Betty, the cousin of a queen someone said, in her espadrilles, laces tied up her freckly legs, would bring a bunch of herbs grown in her terraced garden. She and her husband had a house on the hill, above the puerto, where they spent most of the year.

Once a week, we went into Palma, and sometimes treated ourselves to lunch at El Patio. We usually had the gazpacho, cool and refreshing and simply delicious in a way it seldom is now. On the way back to Andraitx, we would stop at the American library. The books smelled of dusty hot summers, and the librarian, who always wore a white shirt,

sleeves rolled up, and cuffed white trousers, introduced us to books by
Lady Eleanor Smith who wrote about aristocratic English women
rushing off to Spain with gypsies. I read her stories and, much too soon,
those of Dostoevsky and Tolstoy, skipping the battles, in the shade, on a
bleached deck chair, or on my bed in a plain white room. We went to
bullfights. Sometime somewhere we met Antonio Bienvenida. He asked
for my mother's hand, but this was given only in friendship.

Andraitx is too spoiled to return to, but as an adult I have found my
own, and other places. The puerto, as we remember it, exists only in our
thoughts, sometimes on the table, and in my mother's black and white
watercolours on the wall above my bed.

As the months swell towards summer, I think of white-washed walls,
leading the gaze up to terracotta-tiled roofs and to that unique blue of
the Mediterranean sky. It is a thought without melancholy, but if it is
raining outside, I doggedly transpose it into dinner. We eat more fish. I
make a bourride. We have rice salads, the most fruit-like tomatoes I can
find, basil, tarragon, olives, and olive oil which seems to taste stronger
because of the time of year. Hot ratatouille; then cold, adding a little
vinegar which suits the difference of temperature; mashed olives and
aubergine on a hot baguette; a bread-based and fiery aïoli to have with
anything at all; little pieces of squid, cooked with saffron, and later
tossed into a salad of lettuce and tiny courgettes, and if not their own
flowers, then those of nasturtium. Salami, chorizo, and jambon de
Bayonne, which exports with more taste than prosciutto; a salad of
peppers and Mediterranean prawns.

Calamares Andraitx

A simple, delicious meal, easily made ahead of time. It gets better
every day. For four people use 1½–2lb / 675–900g SQUID,
cleaned; 1 LEEK, 3 sweet RED PEPPERS, 4 cloves GARLIC,
chopped; two 14oz / 400g tins Italian plum TOMATOES or
2lb / 900g fresh and peeled tomatoes, chopped; 2 tablespoons
TOMATO PURÉE; a handful PINE NUTS, toasted; 1 BAY
LEAF; ½ teaspoon each CUMIN, ALLSPICE; pinch SAFFRON;
strip ORANGE PEEL; a handful Niçoise BLACK OLIVES.

Prepare the squid, cutting in rings and shortening the tentacles.
Wash the leek and chop quite finely. Start with the squid. On a
medium heat warm enough OLIVE OIL in a cast iron pan to coat
the bottom. Cook the squid until browned, stirring. Add the
tomato purée, dilute with a glass of VERMOUTH or WHITE

WINE, deglazing and scraping up the browned solids on the bottom of the pan. Lower the heat, simmer until the squid begins to stick to the pan, juices reduced. Add another glass of white wine, and repeat the same process.

While the squid cooks, in another large pan cook the leek and garlic in OLIVE OIL, gently, until just softening. Add the spices, orange peel, crushed bay leaf, the pine nuts and the peppers, seeded and cut in strips. Cook until the peppers start to burn. Add the tomatoes and a glass of MADEIRA, then the squid. Simmer, uncovered, for 45 minutes or until reduced by half. Taste, adjust to your liking with freshly ground pepper and salt. Serve with fresh chopped PARSLEY and the black olives.

Squid Risotto without Ink

The ink sac is seldom kept by the fishmonger. Although the taste of ink cannot be substituted, the use of red wine with olive paste and allspice brings a deep colour and taste.

Have ready a cleaned and small SQUID, tentacles and body cut into bite-sized pieces. Cook a few SHALLOTS in OLIVE OIL until soft, add the squid pieces and toss together, on medium heat, until the squid starts to stick and caramelise. Add a dozen CHERRY TOMATOES, 1 tablespoon each of TOMATO PURÉE and OLIVE PASTE, a pinch of ALLSPICE and CAYENNE, a ladleful of FISH STOCK. Simmer until the liquid reduces and, once again, the squid caramelises. Cover with 1½ pint / 900ml fish stock and 2 glasses of RED WINE. Simmer gently for 15 minutes.

Start cooking the rice, adding ladles of the squid and stock as necessary (see page 7).

Serve sprinkled with fresh PARSLEY and as much finely chopped CHILLI PEPPER as you can bear.

Gazpacho El Patio

This should be prepared a day ahead of time and refrigerated, only served on a hot day, as it was to us 30 years ago by the Andalusian chef of El Patio. This is his recipe, scribbled on the edge of our tablecloth, kept safely all these years by my mother in the back of her notebook. It will serve 8 to 10 people.

2 pints / 1 litre water; 1¼lb / 500g WHITE BREADCRUMBS; 1¼lb / 500g TOMATOES; 10oz / 250g GREEN PEPPERS; 10oz / 250g CUCUMBER; 3 cloves GARLIC; 2 heaped table-spoons MAYONNAISE; SALT, OLIVE OIL, VINEGAR to taste.

Save the last 3 ingredients. Put the rest through a mouli, adding the water and, to taste, the olive oil, vinegar and salt. Leave to rest in the fridge for at least 24 hours. Serve with freshly ground PEPPER, just a little chopped cucumber and green pepper on the side, and perhaps a few CROÛTONS. More than this is really not necessary.

This version is thick and quite pale. I use about a third less breadcrumbs and half a green pepper, making up the difference with RED PEPPERS for colour.

La Tour d'Argent; a long birthday

When I was eight, I left New York with my cousin Miguel. We called him Le Moustique. He was two years younger than I and his skin was the colour of my freckles. At the airport, then Idlewild, we were given paper necklaces spelling name and destination. Madrid. Travelling alone on aeroplanes was a habit acquired early. I spent a year in Madrid. I went to the Lycée and was inexplicably converted to Catholicism by the Spanish maid (I had been baptised an Episcopalian in New York) who thought parsley was poison. Miguel's mother, my father's sister, arrived from Brazil, and no longer between planes and husbands, took Miguel to Geneva where she would spend fifteen years with her Swiss husband. At the end of my school year my mother left Spain, ill, broke and worried, to define another life in Paris. I went to live with her sister and brother-in-law in Strasbourg. That lasted six years. During that time my mother came to stay when she could; there were the Andraitx holidays.

The paper necklaces were now seven years behind and during that time I saw my father once, but there were occasional phone calls, and little letters: 'Dear Daddy. I loved the picture of you in the jungle, and your beard. Have you found any gold yet? How are you? I miss you. I'm having a lovely time at school and I have a boyfriend. His name is Denis de Lapparent. I would love some pocket money. Love and kisses.'

My father was a mysterious and coveted figure. He could be relied upon not to be there when expected. Minutes of his presence had to last for years. My mother's side of the family questioned his influence and ways and, while under-age, I was kept from seeing him for fear I wouldn't return, or if I should, do so unrecognizably.

Finally, a meeting was arranged, rather like a disreputable business deal. Three days in Paris. He would arrive from New York, I would arrive from Strasbourg. I was eleven. We shared a big bed in a small hotel in St Germain called Le Montana, across the street from Le Bilboquet where I vaguely remember seeing Juliette Greco, before her street nose had been remodelled to a drawing room nose, singing in her voice of olive oil lyrics written by Sartre and Prévert. Day and night lasted much longer than twenty-four hours. We had drinks and lunches in bars and restaurants that belonged to friends, champagne for my father and a mimosa for me were on the house; we took naps; we went out to dinner and to night clubs; we returned to our room, naughty and almost satisfied, at four in the morning. He drove a fast car through the streets, parking and stepping out of the Ferrari or Maserati in one same movement. He wore suits that were seamed invisibly and there was a silk handkerchief in his breast pocket. He wore suede boots that were made for him in Ecuador. From his belt hung a gold key chain, forming a lazy curve to his pocket where keys rested for doors in funny places, along with his mascot: a small gold nugget, found in a tributary of the Amazon. On his right hand, he wore a signet ring, designed by him, of a Bugatti fender, two crossed fencing swords (he was, at eighteen, the champion of his school, or could it have been France), and the motto Semper Velocissimo. He never crossed a street at the lights. He whistled a jazzy tune, most often 'It Was Just One Of Those Things', and sang 'Sweet Sue', changing the words to 'J'ai Bu Un Pernod, et Trois Curaçaos, J'Suis Saoul, J'Suis Saoul'.

One of those three days in Paris was my birthday. By then, eleven years and eleven schools had passed. For the evening of my twelfth birthday, we went to La Tour d'Argent. The owner, Claude Terrail, was an old friend, from la deuxième guerre. We sat by the window, overlooking 'toutes mes dames' as Claude said, pointing to Notre-Dame and the statues of Sainte Geneviève and Sainte Clothilde. Towards the end of the meal, I was beginning to feel emotionally and gastronomically screwed down. A cake arrived, delivered by Claude, the candle flames blown backwards like yellow ribbons. He brought it swiftly, placing it precisely on the centre of the table. I blew out the candles. All the lights went out. In the restaurant and in Paris. The guardian ladies outside disappeared. I burst into tears. In French, that is called la larme facile. I was in the dark, surrounded by attention, waiters, staring guests, Claude and my father, all invisible. They told me to lift the lid of a small wooden box on the table which had a silver plaque engraved La tour d'Argent. As I did, the lights returned. Inside, and outside. I was literally sick with relief and could barely focus on the three-star cake.

The next day, we went shopping. We stopped at the Rouge et Bleu, where my father had shirts made, if days were flush, and I was fitted as well. Later that afternoon, it was time to part. He stood waving from the corner of the Avenue Georges V and the Champs Elysées, or Illusoires, as my mother says. Back to Strasbourg. He cried. The only time I was to see him do so. I don't remember who drove the car.

My father loved to play tricks and surprises and would go to extreme lengths. The first time he 'took me to the movies' I was living with my mother, now separated from my father, in London. We had just settled in a little mews house in Pavilion Road. The future was being planned as secure. I think I was five. A month later, my father appeared and asked if he could take me out for the afternoon. A movie perhaps. We walked out the door, into a taxi, and onto an aeroplane which took us to Paris. There, I went to a convent school and once, on my Sunday out, found myself sitting next to my father in his single-prop grasshopper, doing figure of eights over Paris and Versailles. The château rose at, and above me in terrifying and exciting waves. Even now, the mere thought transfers itself to the palms of my hands. I hear my father saying 'courageuse ma fille, mais pas téméraire'. Decades later, and unexpectedly as usual, he found me in Mallorca with his sister Arlette and her children, pronouncing his arrival by giving the roof of our holiday house in Pollensa several close shaves. The first pass made us all run out to see who the lunatic was. After the second pass, which flattened us on the grass, we knew. When he walked in, my grandmother said, 'Ah, te voilà, mon fils.'

A year or two after the London kidnapping and the upside down view of Paris, my father and I returned to New York, via Spain and Portugal. Or so I am told. That trip, in the eye of various beholders, is referred to as a 'rescue', a 'surprise', the 'second kidnap'; but I have no recollection of it.

It was to be five years after my twelfth birthday that I would see my father again. And even then he didn't explain how he and Claude Terrail had engineered the set up for the lights at La Tour. As my father often says, 'On s'amuse comme on peut.'

My father read this story the other day. I have, apparently, made two mistakes. The first is that those three days were in fact two weeks. It still feels like three days and not long enough. The second mistake concerns the lighting of public monuments in Paris. They are only fully lit on

Sundays. If you wish to have them completely illuminated during the week, you apply to the municipality for the sector and the hour you choose, for a certain sum. What happened is that, as the lights of La Tour returned, that sector in Paris was floodlit at the same time. My father and Claude, knowing the punctuality of the French, timed the lights of the restaurant to be put out, and returned, accordingly. Truth, as well as beauty, is in the eye of the beholder. I chose to let this story lie as it does in my memory.

Quenelles de Brochet La Tour d'Argent

This is the recipe Claude Terrail sent me, with my translation and with the addition at the end of my father's interpretation which occasionally appears on the menu as Les Quenelles d'Annie, my father's wife.

It is a long and delicate recipe, to serve six to eight.

Remove the skin and bones from a 2¼lb / 1kg PIKE and put twice through a fine sieve or mincer. Put into a bowl over another large bowl filled with ice and water. Fold in 4 beaten EGG WHITES, spoonful by spoonful, working with a wooden spoon. Add SALT and PEPPER. Leave to rest for 2 hours over the ice.

Add, slowly, 2¾ pints / 1.5 litres of CRÈME FRAÎCHE, stirring constantly until you have a homogeneous mixture.

Heat the oven to 200°C 400°F / gas mark 6. BUTTER generously a large oven-proof dish or baking tin. Using a spoon, form the fish mixture into small sausage-like shapes. Place the quenelles delicately into the baking tin. Bring to the boil 3½ pints / 2l of water seasoned with sea salt; add to the quenelles carefully. Poach the quenelles in the oven for 35 minutes without letting the water boil. Adjust the temperature if necessary.

While the quenelles are cooking, prepare the MUSHROOMS, Remove the stalks from 1¾lb / 750g mushrooms. Wash rapidly, dry gently and chop finely. Immediately add the juice of 1 LEMON. Peel and finely chop 4 SHALLOTS.

Heat 2½oz / 60g of butter in a heavy saucepan. Add the shallots. Stir for 2 minutes without letting them colour; add the mushrooms. Cook 4 to 5 minutes at medium heat, stirring constantly as the mixture dries. Add SALT and PEPPER to taste and 8 fl oz / 225ml of the crème fraîche. Stir for another 5 minutes at a more gentle heat, then set aside.

The sauce   Melt 2oz / 50g BUTTER in a heavy saucepan. Add 2oz / 50g FLOUR, stir for 2 to 3 minutes at a gentle heat, pour in 2 fl oz / 50ml MILK all at once, whisking. Season with a generous pinch of NUTMEG, SALT and PEPPER. Let the sauce thicken for 5 minutes while stirring. Remove from heat. Incorporate 3oz / 75g grated GRUYÈRE and leave to rest.

To assemble   Remove the baking tin from the oven. Using a slotted spoon, take out the quenelles and leave to drain on a cloth or paper towels. Heat the grill. BUTTER generously a large, oval gratin dish with 1oz / 25g butter. Spread the mushrooms over the bottom. Arrange the quenelles over the mushrooms. Pour over the sauce. Sprinkle with 4oz / 100g of grated GRUYÈRE. Place the dish under the grill. Leave for 7 to 8 minutes, until well gratiné, or browned. Serve immediately.

My father's rendition   Instead of a sauce Mornay, he prepares a beurre blanc, using a WHITE WINE such as Mâcon or Sancerre, reduced with a drop of VINEGAR, fresh DILL or ground FENNEL, fresh BASIL. Then he whisks in the butter with a little CRÈME FRAÎCHE. He sprinkles over the quenelles a grated mixture of two parts GRUYÈRE to one part finely crumbled STILTON.

　　If pike is difficult to find, substitute SOLE, TROUT, HALIBUT or TURBOT.

Mummy's Cake

This is a cake my mother used to make on my birthday; it is now a cake I make on my children's birthdays, which means it has been referred to, for at least thirty years, as Mummy's Cake. It is almost what the French call Quatre-Quarts or the Americans a Pound Cake, in which weight of sugar and butter matches the weight of eggs, the weight of flour being the equal of the first three. Our version is a more moist cake, almost a Baba sans Rhum.

It is simple to do, especially if you have a Magimix. I have made it by hand and by machine and once, the day after food poisoning, trying to shut off all my senses at the mere sight and thought of food. As a result, I didn't measure or mix particularly thoroughly, but the cake was good nevertheless. I have also frozen it (without icing) with good results. It will feed 8 to 10 people.

Pre-heat oven to 150°C / 300°F / gas mark 2. Mix well 9oz / 225g softened BUTTER with 12oz / 300g granulated SUGAR; add 13oz / 325g white FLOUR, 1½ level teaspoons BAKING POWDER, a pinch of SALT. Combine until evenly crumbly. Grate the skin of 1 LEMON (or orange) into the mixture, using the less fine side of the grater. Beat 6 EGGS with a fork, add 3 teaspoons VANILLA ESSENCE and pour into the cake mixture.

Butter a cake tin thoroughly, preferably hinged, removable bottom, 8–9in / 20–25cm in diameter, 3in / 7.5cm deep. Line the bottom with buttered greaseproof paper. Pour the batter into the cake tin, bake 45 minutes to an hour, or until a knife comes out not quite clean or dry. Leave to cool for a few minutes. Run a knife around the edges, release the hinge and remove the cake to a serving dish. Slice the cake in half, horizontally. Pour onto both sides the juice of 2 LEMONS mixed with 1 tablespoon of SUGAR. Close the cake. When completely cool, make an icing to your liking.

Instead of the lemon juice, make a syrup of LEMON JUICE and SUGAR, lightly caramelised.

Or, melt 3 or 4 tablespoons of a seedless jam, such as redcurrant or damson, with a glass of crème de cassis. Bubble for a moment, pour onto the cake. I sometimes drop a handful of fresh raspberries into the cassis syrup and use the raspberries on top of the cake, glazed by the syrup.

Or, serve plain with a Sabayon sauce (see page 6), a fresh fruit salad on the side.

Or, my favourite: pour a red wine sauce over the cake like that for Poires au Cassis (see page 31).

September

... and now Georgia reminds me
that "Grandaddy did his finger
dance..."

A new address; McDonald's hamburgers on the floor; dancing to memory

We were moving to a new house in Fulham in six weeks' time. I took possession on the 26th of this month. At seven that evening the children and I sat on the floor in the sitting room of the empty house, a naked bulb hanging from the ceiling, sipping red wine between bites of a McDonald's hamburger, French fries and peaches. All that was left in the house was a dull beige on walls, curtains and floor. We were euphoric.

'But can we change the colour of the walls, Mummy?' Tasha asked a little anxiously. I promised the house would be full of light by November and then we would have a christening party. We went upstairs to choose bedrooms by way of a secret ballot. I was relieved to see from the folded paper votes in my hat that they hadn't chosen the same room. The coin in my hand wouldn't need to be tossed after all. It was a beautiful day, a clear sky and warm air. The summer months had been cold and disappointing but friends, time and events were frenzied and I didn't notice. Now we were having an Indian summer but I was clashing anxiety with excitement. Tasha was twelve. This would be her fifth move. Georgia, three years younger, would be punching one move less on her clock. She was dancing on the terracotta tiled kitchen floor. 'Listen! My shoes make such a good noise.' Tasha had brought her portable cassette player and put on a tape of Louis Armstrong. The strains of C'Est Si Bon wafted through the house bringing images of my father. I heard the sound of change in his pocket as he took two steps at a time up the staircase of many and forgotten houses, whistling the same tune. [A driving lesson in Ecuador when I was eighteen – his instructions: 'change down for that corner, rev up between changes, that's it, now accelerate, hold it like a flower, easy'; tasting a sauce, holding the wooden spoon between his teeth like a rose, twirling his wife Annie into a dramatic tango backward pass, after which the phrase 'mm, Mademoiselle, vous habitez chez vos parents?' And then he was gone: 'see you next time I meet you.']

He and his wife came to stay one autumn and Indian summer at Beaver Dam, arriving from France with four friends de passage. They were armed with one fresh foie gras, two truffles collected the previous day from the land of a friend's farm in the Périgord, and breathing the memory of an extraordinary bottle of Calvados Hors d'Age regrettably forgotten on the plane. We started lunch with drinks on the lawn; later we returned to the lawn, under the trees, leaving two bottles of Miles' vintage port standing empty on the table. After a nap under an oak tree they decided it was time to 'secouer les vieilles branches avec un jeu de paume'. We called up some friends and spilled onto their tennis court a few minutes later. The plan was executed literally. Lightheaded, they ran in their bare feet in bumper car patterns, hitting the ball with the palms of their hands.

That day three of us had cooked lunch. I prepared a camembert en brioche. My father cooked his veau au porto and Annie made her gâteau à l'orange. The goose liver was put into a marinade for the next day. And now Georgia reminds me that 'Granddaddy did his finger dance.' This is how it works: close your hands into two fists. Hold them two inches above the table, facing each other. Drop down second and fourth fingers from each hand, like two pairs of legs. Then thumbs and little fingers lift up to join each other. Now you have a couple holding hands, doing a paso doble around the peppermill and salad bowl.

Camembert en Chemise

Paula Wolfert published this recipe several years ago in an American magazine called the Pleasures of Cooking, crediting a young chef by the name of Jeremy Ungar. I can no longer find the original, but I think this is a faithful reproduction. It is far more simple and pleasant to execute than the description implies. It is delicious. For six to eight:

Prepare a BRIOCHE DOUGH one day in advance. Roll out into a 12in / 30cm round. Place an 8oz / 200g CAMEMBERT, unpasteurized, just ripe, crust removed, in the middle of the circle of dough, pick up the sides and overlap over the cheese. Pinch the edges of dough and seal with EGG glaze.

Seamside down, turn onto a BUTTERED, shallow 8in / 20cm round baking dish. Cover with foil and leave aside for 1–2 hours in a warm, damp place.

Heat oven to hot, put dish on top shelf and bake 10 minutes. Bring down to the middle shelf, drop the heat to medium and bake another 10 minutes. Let it rest a few minutes, serve warm, sprinkled with freshly ground pepper and fresh parsley or chives.

Brioche dough　Dissolve ¾ teaspoon DRIED YEAST (1 whole teaspoon in winter) in 2 tablespoons warm MILK with a pinch of SUGAR. Put this into a large bowl or Magimix, add 2oz / 50g of FLOUR, one EGG. Combine well. Sprinkle 4oz / 100g FLOUR over the mixture but do not stir it in. Cover the bowl, put aside for 1–2 hours at room temperature.

Add 2 tablespoons of SUGAR, ½ teaspoon of SALT and 1 EGG to the mixture. Stir and combine well. Slowly add 4oz / 100g BUTTER in small pieces. Incorporate thoroughly. Place this mixture in a large bowl, with enough room for it to rise, and sprinkle lightly with flour. Cover tightly with cling film and leave to rise at room temperature for 3–4 hours, until it has tripled in size and seems spongy. It may take 1–2 hours longer in winter.

Deflate the dough with a wooden spoon or plastic scraper, stirring it down. Cover and refrigerate until firm, about 15 minutes. Turn onto a floured board. Flour your hands, spread the dough into a rectangle 9 × 5in / 22 × 12cm. Fold gently into thirds. Turn the dough 90 degrees, spread out once again and fold into three. Dust the dough with flour, wrap in cling film and leave in fridge overnight.

Delicatessens; a new friend

A delicatessen should be reliable for local news, for small délicatesses or forget-me-nots in the kitchen – olive paste, tiny capers, fresh black olives and a few specialities made by the family running the store. In Westchester, I went to Joe's. I would find fresh mozzarella made by his brother in the back kitchen, immersed in salted or unsalted water to suit different customers' tastes; sausages made with fennel seeds and Parmesan, or allspice, Cayenne and garlic; bacalhau from September to April which came, unexpectedly, from Canada; plain pancetta, or rolled with mozzarella, delicious melted on toast; and the near equivalent of the French saucisson de Lyon called Cotechino (it appears here in a box: don't buy it), its pronunciation distorted by the second generation of Italian immigrants into codeghin. These swung from the ceiling with salamis, chorizo, prosciutto and Smithfield hams. The best ham, sweet and smoked over corn cobs, came from Harrington's in Vermont. There was a branch in Connecticut, forty minutes away from the house, to which I went every two or three months. I would return with an eight to ten pound ham, a few bone ends for soup and preservative-free bacon. The leftovers of the roast ham were ground, put into small foil packets and frozen. A handful of this delicate and perfect meat gave a wonderful scent to risotto, soup, scrambled eggs or spaghetti.

In London, I am fickle, I spread my allegiance. If I have an appointment near Soho I drop in on my Spanish delicatessen in Charlotte Street to buy his olive oil, almond oil, perhaps a little Serrano ham (Andalusian ham, mountain-cured, better than imported prosciutto), a chorizo, or membrillo (quince cheese) for the children. In Fulham Road, I find pecorino, Parmesan, olive paste, the small capers and jars of cuttlefish for last minute salads and last minute guests. Tarfa, a friend whose name means everlasting tree ('I will never live up to it,' she says, adding 'there are no roots') introduced me to a Lebanese delicatessen owner who really does make his own hummus, green olives dressed in coriander seeds, lemon, garlic and olive oil, and has a pungent cheese the Lebanese nibble between courses in the spirit of the French who, sometimes, in the middle of a meal, have a barely sweetened sorbet to clear the palate – a trou normand.

Salted cod, mozzarella made in the back kitchen, and cotechino are elusive. My search continues, with Tarfa's help. Our friendship feels a decade old, but we only met a year ago. She pointed this out to me the other day, explaining that this would not have happened had we met 'in English'. Although she is eloquently fluent, we crossed over into French almost immediately which gave us a humour and emotion that in translation would have lost its intimacy and colour.

Mozzarella Salad
In order of preference:
'La Mozzarella' (quote marks are on the packet), a blue and white lettered packet weighing 5oz / 125g, made in Polenghi, Italy. Made from cow's milk and sits in brine in the packet. It has a light skin and is buttery, as long as the shop you buy it from does not keep it in a refrigerator. The usual cool cheese shelf is fine.

Mozzarella di Bufala – a white and green packet. Made in Italy with buffalo milk. A little grainy, not firm enough to toss in a mixed salad, unless very carefully; a slightly soured taste.

Mozzarella – a red and green packet. Made by Carnevale in North London – the most commonly available. Rubbery, holds if tossed but not so good as other two.

Whichever you buy, use them within a day or two, store them in a cool place but not in the refrigerator – a temperature that cold hardens the texture and the butteriness will be lost.

Slice the MOZZARELLA into 1/4in / 6mm thick slices. Lay decoratively on a platter. Toss lightly, until a little browned, 2 tablespoons of slivered ALMONDS mixed with 2 tablespoons of CORIANDER seeds, in a small frying pan just coated with ALMOND or OLIVE OIL. Let the mixture cool a little, then add a few tablespoons of good olive oil with a dash of VINEGAR or LEMON JUICE. Pour over the mozzarella just a few seconds before serving, then add SALT and freshly ground PEPPER and chopped PARSLEY. The warmth of the dressing will bring out the taste of the olive oil further and the mozzarella will seem even more buttery.

Variations   Circle the mozzarella with RED PEPPERS, finely sliced and quickly stir fried, burning them just a little.

Cube the mozzarella, toss in a salad of AVOCADO, burnt PEPPERS, FRISÉE LETTUCE and CROÛTONS.

Saucisson de Toulouse or Cotechino

In America, I could not find the Toulouse or Lyon sausages. Instead, I used the Italian Cotechino, the name often distorted beyond recognition, from codeghini to gudaghini to goleghino. Here it is the opposite. I have not been successful in finding the Cotechino. Do not buy the ones some Italian delicatessens sell, sealed in foil and packaged in boxes from Italy. The French sausages are available in Soho and from London's French butchers. They usually weigh about 1 1/2lb / 725g and are rich enough to serve 4 people. I have found here Saucisse de Morteau, made in the Franche Comté. Smaller, weighing about 8oz / 225g, it is delicious and quite strong.

Place the SAUCISSON DE TOULOUSE OR LYON (usually pork, sometimes mixed with beef, or veal spiced according to each region's whim and butcher's ability) in an oval gratin dish, about 2in / 5cm deep. Prick lightly with a fork, pour over a bottle of robust RED WINE. Scatter CLOVES, a pinch each of ALLSPICE, GROUND FENNEL or CUMIN, a broken BAY

LEAF. Simmer for 30 minutes, maintaining the level of liquid with a little water. Turn the saucisson 2 or 3 times. Leave to rest in the liquor until you are ready to serve. Slice on the bias with small NEW POTATOES tossed in warmed OLIVE OIL, a little MUSTARD and fresh CHIVES and PARSLEY.

You can use a little of the liquor spooned over each helping. The rest adds a wonderful taste to gravies, soup or stock. Store in jam jars and freeze. The fat will rise; use this instead of butter for sautéeing potatoes.

Joe's Salt Cod

Joe's salt cod was plump and came in fillets – few bones, no skin. Only use this recipe if you find the same quality, and please tell me if you do, as, so far, I have not succeeded in finding it.

Soak the SALT COD for twenty-four hours in cold water, changing the water three or four times. Blanch the fish for 5 minutes in simmering water. Taste the fish; if it seems very salty, blanch a further few minutes. Drain, separate into manageable portions.

Soften gently in OLIVE OIL, sliced ONIONS, chopped GARLIC, YELLOW or RED PEPPERS. Add TOMATOES. Cook for 10 minutes, add WHITE WINE and CHICKEN STOCK, thickened with two hard-boiled yolks of EGG and if you have it, a ladle of bourride. Simmer another 10 minutes. Taste for seasoning. If bourride stock not available, adjust with a little TOMATO PURÉE, ALLSPICE and GROUND FENNEL. The sauce should be almost as thick as single cream.

Lay half the sauce in a gratin dish, then the pieces of salt cod. Add the rest of the sauce to cover. Glaze in a hot oven until the dish begins to caramelise, about 15 minutes. Serve sprinkled with fresh PARSLEY and grated PARMESAN.

No game in America; shopping in a garage; Christmas pudding in Beaver Dam; the coffee explodes

The month of September in America brought on the search for game. The rules of the Food and Health Administration are that pheasant or duck are domesticated birds and never hung. Wild game cannot be sold by butchers; should you bring in a wild bird, the butcher will refuse to pluck it. At first, I used marinades to achieve a gamy taste with lamb or pork. I found that just a tablespoon of Roquefort in the gravy was sufficient to give pungency to the sauce for a leg of lamb without the source being obvious, and only detectable with hindsight. A loin of pork, marinated for four or five days in red wine, with juniper berries and bourbon, became gently gamy.

Then, one day, our Fiat broke down and I took it to a garage that serviced foreign cars. The owner was a short, energetic and slightly bad-tempered Frenchman. While he lay under the car, I sat on a faded and torn thing that must have once been a sofa, and chatted. His name was Alain Rossignol, he had lived in America for twenty-odd years and would never consider returning to France except for the occasional holiday. Nevertheless, he listened to Charles Aznavour all day, and missed le gibier. Two or three times a winter he would go into the Westchester woods and hunt deer, using a battery-powered bow and arrow that stood an inch or two taller than he. There was a small fridge in the corner of his garage where he kept his catch, divided into various cuts, allotted according to la tête du client. I asked him to put me on the list of the better têtes and, for the remaining three years of our life in Katonah, I had a reliable supply of venison and, occasionally, a duck or pheasant. My purchase became a ritual. I would arrive late in the morning, to be given a washed-out Amora mustard pot 'glass' half filled with red wine and a piece of cheese. We would talk as he fiddled with engines, strong smells of petrol, of brake fluid, of wine and cheese, wafting past and clashing pleasantly. He had a friend who grew sorrel, impossible to find in American vegetable markets at the time and this was added to my basket. I no longer needed to use my substitute combination of spinach and mint when I had a craving for the taste of potage à l'oseille.

And, if I hadn't already done so, the children would remind me it was time to make the Christmas pudding. This was a tradition we all joined in. The recipe came from Susan, my mother-in-law. Each month we would examine the puddings, usually one large and two small, pour a little brandy over each and return them to the larder having taken a good whiff but resisted the urge to scrape off just a bit from the top. Susan's instructions were 'This is a perfect recipe, doesn't need any funny French nonsense added to it,' so I resisted the urge and she was right. Susan would arrive in time for a last inspection a few days before Christmas, with a big smile on her face, a suitcase full of presents and a pair of well-hung grouse.

One week-end we had had ten people for lunch outside. Barbecued pork chops and ears of corn gently charred and so much more that I have now forgotten, but I remember the feeling of satisfaction bordering on the too-much. Miles took our guests for a walk after lunch and I remained behind, officially to tidy up, but in reality 'pour prendre une petite sieste avec mon digestif', as my father says. I had just reached the bedroom door when I heard Miles returning. My heart sank as unknown voices seemed to have joined his and those of our guests. The new voices belonged to two Italian couples who had lost themselves in our woods. They sat down, silk scarves and fine suede jackets left in the hall. We offered them coffee while giving them directions to their host's house, a mile's walk away along the stream below. They talked among themselves while struggling with us in pidgin English. 'La casa e simpatica, no? La moglie e molto Inglese; il marito pare Tedesco.' [The house is cosy. The wife is very English; the husband looks German.] I came in with the coffee, pleased by the first comment, put out by the second. Distracted and holding back my understanding of Italian, I pushed down the plunger of the glass cafetière too soon. The pot exploded. Coffee and bits of glass flew. Into the fireplace, onto the carpet. Splattering Gucci boots and someone's silver- coloured corduroys. Since everyone found this rather amusing, I left them to it and went to make yet more coffee. Finally, they had their coffee, exclaiming 'ottimo ottimo' [the best] and Miles, now heading a crowd of fourteen, took them all into the woods again. Revved up by events I soon followed.

I don't often use my present cafetière, although when I do I remember to wait for the pocket of air beneath the plunger to escape. I dislike intensely the gadgets people use to make their coffee. They look like robots or tanks. Most days, I simply follow the Turkish system without making it quite so strong or thick. As for tea, I pour boiling water over the coffee grounds, in an earthenware jug. Two or three stirs of the spoon, a few seconds' rest and then pour the coffee through a fine sieve into the cup. I have yet to find a system that works any faster or that tastes as good. Six heaped tablespoons to just over 1 ½ pints / 900ml of water.

Christmas Pudding

The tradition is to make this 6 months in advance, even one year. But some years galloped ahead of me and, once or twice, I made the pudding late, at the end of November, even early December. Nevertheless, the pudding was always just right. The recipe was given to me by my mother-in-law. My only change, over the years, has been to intensify the spices.

You will need 8oz / 225g each of CURRANTS, SULTANAS, RAISINS, WHITE BREADCRUMBS, freshly made, crust removed, DARK BROWN SUGAR. 6oz / 150g mixed CANDIED PEEL or, if you prefer, LEMON and ORANGE PEEL; 4oz / 100g blanched and slivered ALMONDS, lightly toasted; 8oz / 225g SELF-RAISING FLOUR, 8oz / 225g shredded SUET, 1 good pinch SALT, 1oz / 25g MIXED SPICE; 1 teaspoon each NUTMEG, ALLSPICE, MACE, CINNAMON; 1 LEMON, juice and grated peel; 8oz / 225g dark, coarse cut MARMALADE; 6 EGGS; ½ pint / 300ml GUINNESS; BRANDY.

Mix thoroughly all dry ingredients. Add grated lemon peel, juice of lemon, marmalade and beaten eggs. Gradually add half the stout, stir well. Cover with a cloth and leave overnight.

Add the rest of the stout, stirring well. Mix in 2 tablespoons of brandy (or dark rum for a change). Turn into well buttered pudding basins, the mixture reaching three quarters of the way up each bowl. Cover with buttered, greaseproof paper, then foil, making a pleat of each across the top. Tie securely with string. Steam steadily for 4 hours. Cool, store in a dark and cool place.

Check once a month, prick the top of the pudding and sprinkle on a tablespoon of brandy. Cover again with clean foil.

On Christmas Day, change the cover, using again pleated buttered greaseproof paper and foil. Tie with string. Steam for 2 hours, maintaining the level of water half way up the pudding basin. Decant onto a serving dish, serve with a warmed ladle of brandy, ignited over the pudding.

This quantity will make two large puddings, enough for 6 to 8 per pudding, and one little pudding for 2 to 4.

Rôti de Porc Faisandé

Until I found a source for game in America, this was my way of producing meat tasting gamy, inspired by Elizabeth David, stretched to my own taste.

For a roast of about 5lb/2.25kg in weight, enough for 8 to 10 people, prepare the following marinade:

Half a bottle of robust RED WINE, simmered for 10 minutes

with 4 tablespoons good SHERRY or CIDER VINEGAR; 3 cloves chopped GARLIC; 2 broken BAY LEAVES; a dozen PEPPER-CORNS, a dozen crushed JUNIPER BERRIES; a pinch of SALT; a generous shot each of GIN (Gordon's) and BOURBON. Cool, then pour over the pork placed in a dish just large enough to hold the meat and at least 2in / 5cm deep. Prick the meat all over, turn several times in the marinade, leave in a cool place covered with a cloth for at least two days, four being even better.

Remove the meat, pat dry and place in an oiled roasting pan. Strain the marinade and reserve. Roast the pork in a hot oven for 20 minutes. Turn the heat down to medium, pour the strained marinade over the meat. Baste the meat every 15 minutes, letting the gravy evaporate and caramelise at the sides of the pan, before adding more red wine, a little water or STOCK. Half way through, thicken with a dessertspoonful of strong Dijon MUSTARD. When done, transfer the sauce to a saucepan, reduce or adjust to your taste. Leave the meat to rest in the oven for at least 15 minutes, heat turned off, door left ajar.

I treat a leg of lamb in the same way, adding a teaspoonful of Roquefort mashed into a ladle of marinade, then added to the meat while it roasts.

Potage Faute de Mieux

This was my way of satisfying, almost, a craving for sorrel soup, before I found a source. For four people soften a large, finely chopped ONION in BUTTER in a deep large saucepan. Add 2oz / 50g of Arborio RICE; stir a minute in the butter and onions. Pour in 1½–2 pints / 900–1100ml rich CHICKEN BROTH and a handful of roughly chopped CELERIAC. Simmer uncovered until the rice is cooked. Add 8oz / 225g well rinsed SPINACH, shredded. Simmer covered for 2 minutes. Remove the vegetables with a slotted spoon to a mouli or Magimix, blend to a purée with a more than generous handful of fresh MINT LEAVES. Return to the broth.

Season with SALT, freshly ground PEPPER, a dash of LEMON JUICE, a little SINGLE CREAM and BUTTER.

WATERCRESS can be used instead of the spinach, cooked in the same way, until just wilted.

Potage à l'Oseille Rossignol

I still think of Alain Rossignol under a car in his garage when I make this soup. For four people melt 1 large ONION, chopped, in 4 or 5 tablespoons of BUTTER, in a large saucepan. Stir and cook gently until wilted. Don't let it brown. Add 1lb / 450g of POTATOES, peeled and diced. Stir for a minute, cover with 2 pints / 1.1 litres of CHICKEN STOCK. Simmer until the potatoes are cooked. Add a generous handful, about 6oz / 150g, of washed and shredded SORREL leaves, preferably young ones. Simmer, covered for 4 to 5 minutes. Remove the vegetables with a slotted spoon to a mouli or Magimix. Purée almost finely. Return to the broth. Taste for seasoning. You may need a dash of SUGAR, then SALT and freshly ground PEPPER. Add a little SINGLE CREAM or MILK, a good knob of BUTTER.

I often make this for a winter Sunday supper, thickened with a cupful of leftover LENTILS or FLAGEOLETS, a few diced slices of SAUCISSON, then sprinkled with PARMESAN.

Philosophy in the kitchen

Feeling confused today; here I go again, philosophy in the kitchen, head crowded with people all talking at once, interrupting; a flash of sitting on the terrace of the Café Miramar, a night thirty years ago, my mother and cousin Miguel, sky and stars, a conversation about the cosmos and life; it is going to rain, again; what to have for dinner; there's a man on a roof across the street, fixing tiles. Stop. This must be a day to make soup.

I had some stock left made from marrow bones and the end of a leg of lamb. I bought a handful of spinach, two tiny courgettes, leeks, carrots and celery. The rest was in the cupboard. Minestrone à la Morland and Toby was coming to dinner. Then Miles called: 'may I invite myself to an EGD?' – an acronym for Exceptionally Good Dinner that I sometimes dreaded. 'If you are still in that business,' he continued. The children were delighted and I told them that ex-husbands can make the best of friends. I chopped onions, carrots, celery, to a fine mirepoix, and sweated this until almost soft in olive oil. Then I fried a handful of minced meat separately and added it to the mirepoix. 'Can't you marry a best friend?' a young voice behind me asked. I couldn't think of an answer just then. 'Tell you tomorrow,' I said, scraping up the bottom of the frying pan with a little stock, then half a bottle of red wine, the rest of the stock, four medium potatoes, cubed, a small tin of tomatoes, half a tin of tomato purée, six whole cloves of garlic for crushing in the spoon later, when at table. Georgia laid the table and didn't ask any more questions. I turned the heat down, seasoned the soup with three teaspoons of my special mixture in the peppermill: allspice berries, black and white and red peppercorns, coriander seeds. Then a teaspoon of anchovy paste and one of harissa, diluted first in a bowl, with a spoon of the minestrone. The soup would simmer, covered, for an hour. I went upstairs to have a bath. Those noisy people in my head had calmed down and I looked forward to dinner.

I added chopped leeks and the courgettes, put them in the soup, left it to simmer another five minutes, then turned the heat off. Just before serving, I put in the handful of shredded spinach, just as much parsley, brought the soup up to a near boil. At table, we would dribble a little fresh olive oil, and grate fresh Parmesan, over our bowls. The rest of dinner was only salad of watercress, cos lettuce and spring onions, then cheese. 'No pudding?' the children asked, knowing I seldom make one but, sensing I was malleable coaxed me into it. I quickly made a caramel sauce, thinned with lemon juice, rosewater, just a little boiling water. I poured this over sliced bananas and let them wilt in the heat of the sauce. The scent of rosewater, combined with that strange smell of fresh bananas, increases. As you walk past, it makes you stop to wonder.

Minestrone à la Morland

The following is only a guide, since almost anything goes. Leftover gravy, lentils or flageolets can thicken the body of this soup, not really a minestrone but a first cousin. It makes a satisfying winter lunch or supper; not much more than salad and cheese are wanted afterwards. For six to eight people you will need 2 medium CARROTS; 2 CELERY sticks; 2 medium ONIONS; half a FENNEL bulb; 6–8 GARLIC cloves, whole, peeled; 3 waxy, medium-sized POTATOES, peeled and cubed; 1 large handful minced LAMB; half a bottle RED WINE; 4/5 pint / 1/2 litre rich MEAT STOCK; 1 small tin of whole TOMATOES; 1/2 tin TOMATO PURÉE; 2 teaspoons freshly ground red and white and black PEPPERCORNS, CORIANDER seeds, ALLSPICE berries; handful young SPINACH leaves, washed and shredded; 2 small COURGETTES, unpeeled, sliced lengthwise, then thickly sliced; 2 small LEEKS, washed, sliced lengthwise, then chopped; 1 teaspoon each of ANCHOVY PASTE and HARISSA; OLIVE OIL, freshly grated PARMESAN, PARSLEY.

Brown the meat lightly and reserve. In a large saucepan, sweat the onions, celery, fennel bulb and carrots, finely chopped, in 4 tablespoons good olive oil, for 5–10 minutes, stirring often. Let the mirepoix stick a little to the bottom of the pan as you stir, then scrape it up before it browns. Add the garlic and potatoes. Stir in the tomato, anchovy and harissa pastes, then the meat. Pour in the stock, wine, whole tomatoes and their juice. Break up the tomatoes roughly. Season with the pepper mixture and taste. Perhaps add a bay leaf and a bouquet garni. Cover and simmer gently for at least an hour. Taste again and adjust accordingly. Add a pinch of sugar, salt?

Fifteen minutes before serving, add the chopped leeks, then the courgettes. Simmer covered for 10 minutes, then add the spinach, uncovered. Simmer another 3 to 4 minutes. Add 2 teacups of finely chopped parsley.

At table, dribble a spoonful of olive oil over each bowl and let each person grate Parmesan into the soup.

Caramel Sauce for Fruit, with Rosewater

This is a scented sauce for peaches in summer, bananas or pears in winter. It's also rather good over vanilla ice cream. Children are usually very fond of it. The following will be enough for four people, allowing a peach or a pear per person.

In a heavy saucepan slowly melt 2 teacups of CASTER SUGAR, over medium heat. As caramel appears at the edges of the saucepan, stir in the rest of unmelted sugar. The mixture will go into crumbly lumps, but don't worry. Let it melt further, crushing bits of the hardening sugar with the back of a wooden spoon. Slowly the mass will melt further and begin to turn translucent, liquifying. The colour will become tobacco-ish. Before the colour deepens more than that, stir in half a teaspoon of VINEGAR – this will prevent the caramel from burning as you cook further.

Now add 3 tablespoons of just boiled water and stand back as you do – the caramel will froth and spit. Keep stirring. A mass of caramel will stick to your spoon – never mind – add three more tablespoons of hot water, stirring. After 1 or 2 minutes, the mass will thin, the added water having been incorporated. You will feel rather than see this happening as the mixture will be frothing.

Remove from the heat for a moment. If the mixture seems to thicken too readily, then return to the heat (otherwise, when it cools much more, it will solidify too much). Add 1 or 2 spoonfuls of water; stir and that should do it. Add the juice of half a LEMON and one teaspoon of ROSEWATER (or for a change, ORANGE BLOSSOM WATER). Both are available at most chemists. They are also excellent make-up removers – they feel gentle, fresh and cool on the face at night. Pour immediately over peeled, fresh PEARS – cut into pleasing shapes or just halved. Leave the pears to sit for half a day. They will add their own delicate taste to the caramel. As the sauce cools, taste. Perhaps a little more lemon juice or rosewater?

Peaches benefit from a long soak (peeled and halved or sliced), as the pears do, but the texture of bananas is more delicate and one half-hour soaking is enough.

A little double cream stirred into the caramel will disappear but give the sauce more body, if that is what you feel you'd like that day.

October

... the children and I lived
in enthusiastic squalor. The staircase
was our table...

Moving; postcards; picnic on the stairs; infatuation

We moved to Fulham. On the day, amidst cartons, tea chests, plastic bags, suitcases, movers, painters, plumber, Dougie the electrician – stood Colin, framed in the doorway, holding a bunch of anemones in one hand, a bottle of champagne in the other. He put both on the stairs, embraced me, and embarrassed, rushed off. Being a friend who is an architect, he returned a week later for a free glance at foundations. Chrissie, my sister-in-law, arrived, sat on the same stairs, admired the fabulous mess, wished me luck and left. The florist I used to send myself flowers twice a month at the old address, sent me a bunch at his own cost. My builder for the previous house came, with his mother-in-law who had been my cleaning lady for two years. Cards, another embrace and tears. My soon-to-be-ex-husband sent freesias and daisies.

The next morning, there was mail. It seemed an event to receive any on the first day. It was a postcard. A black and white drawing of a straight road. At the top, was a rear view mirror reflecting the same road. It had to be one of Murray's drawings. It was titled *Déjà Vu*. The message was 'I am sure your future road is bigger than your past!' Each small gesture was a giant moment of pleasure that carried us through the muddle and horror of moving. Then there was a postcard from Robert, wishing us luck in our 'brand new home'. It was to be his last wave. We didn't see him again. I remarked on this, one day, to Tasha. Friends should keep in touch. 'But Mummy, maybe he doesn't feel like it,' she said. A simple and just wisdom.

For ten days, the children and I lived in enthusiastic squalor. The staircase was our table. We sat, one above the other, each to our step laid for a picnic. Sometimes hummus, tapenade, hard-boiled eggs, tabbouleh rich with mint, sardines, tomatoes, spring onions, raw courgettes with my emergency mayonnaise: Hellman's mixed with a tablespoon of plain yoghurt, a tablespoon of Dijon mustard, a little oil, one egg yolk. I thought again of my making mayonnaise in Yorkshire in June, but in this setting Hellman's felt even more of an accomplishment.

And finally, the kitchen was ready. We could sit at table and have a hot meal. I melted butter with parsley, chives and a little cream. We had this over verdure bolliti misti. Then escalopes of pale French veal, cooked in butter, lemon and Madeira. A salad of endives and watercress. Bananas in a butterscotch sauce. Tasha laid the table and lit candles. Georgia made the salad dressing, better than I did. We ate too much, felt a little sick and happy. Kimbers, our black and white cat I think of as a Friesian bull, climbed through the cat door into the newly paved garden. This was a special moment. Tasha got up to watch his progress: 'One paw has touched the ground. Now the other. He is looking right. He is looking left. He is staring at a bush. He is advancing towards the bush. He is behind the bush. He is scratching the ground!' Kimbers, at last, had adjusted to his new address. No more messes on the new carpet. It had taken three weeks. He came back in, jumped up on a counter and sat down, looking vaguely superior.

Late that night, I sat on the stairs, half way up and looked down, admiring my new house. In a month or so, it would be finished. I have never owned anything. I felt the hot folly of infatuation. As you walk in to this house, you see a large room, divided by an open and central staircase. Ahead, down a step, is the kitchen, with a table long enough to seat ten comfortably. I chose the house because of its kitchen. It is big enough to be a social room, which is how kitchens used to be and essential for me. Office, dining room and sitting room. There are sofa and armchairs the other side of the staircase, but when you sit there, you are still a part of the kitchen.

Crème de Pommes Caramelisées

This dessert is always a success, simple to do and a little mysterious. No one is ever quite certain what it is. It can be prepared a day in advance. You will need a ring mould able to hold about 1½ pints / 900ml of liquid.

For six to eight people melt 8oz / 200g of white granulated SUGAR in a heavy saucepan, slowly, without stirring. As it turns to an almost dark tobacco-colour, drop a scant teaspoon of mild VINEGAR into the caramel to prevent it burning. Pour immediately into the mould, unbuttered, tipping it to distribute the caramel evenly. As it hardens, turn upside down over grease-proof paper to encourage it to spread down the sides.

In a heavy, large saucepan, cook 7 medium Granny Smith APPLES, cored, peeled and roughly chopped, with a small glass of semi-sweet WHITE WINE. Stir continuously at high heat. As the apples break into a rough purée, add 4 tablespoons white SUGAR and 7 tablespoons BUTTER, previously melted to the point of turning brown. Add a heaped tablespoonful of JAM, such as crab apple jelly or a not too sweet apricot or damson plum. Remove from the heat. Don't worry about the purée not being perfectly smooth.

Beat in 4 EGGS, one at a time. Pour immediately into the caramelised mould. Sit the mould in a pan filled with hot water which reaches half way up the mould. Bake in a medium oven for 50 minutes to one hour. A knife should come out almost clean, the pudding near firm. Cool to a temperature warm to the hand, then loosen the edges with a blunt knife. To decant, place a large round dish over the mould and turn upside down. Leave the mould to act as a cover and refrigerate.

Serve with crème fraîche or a Sabayon sauce (see page 6) and extra caramel. Melt 8oz / 200g granulated SUGAR as before, add the VINEGAR, then a small teacup of just boiled water with a few drops of fresh LIME juice. This will prevent the caramel from solidifying.

Vinaigrette and Other Dressings

Vinaigrette Start with a good tablespoon of strong Dijon MUSTARD in the salad bowl. Stirring with a wooden spoon, dilute with good VINEGAR (sherry or cider), slowly add OLIVE or PEANUT OIL, stirring vigorously with the wooden spoon. An emulsion will form. Season with SALT and freshly ground PEPPER. I use approximately 2 tablespoons vinegar to 5 tablespoons olive oil.

Variations: half PEANUT OIL, half WALNUT or HAZELNUT OIL; Colman's mustard. Should the emulsion not take, or separate, or should you not want to use mustard but want the oil and vinegar to amalgamate, add just under a teaspoon of EGG YOLK and stir briskly with a wooden spoon.

Dressings for vegetable salads such as: French STRING BEANS, just blanched, tossed with finely sliced ONION and MINT leaves; barely blanched courgettes with fresh TOM-ATOES; blanched CAULIFLOWER, with black OLIVES and

ANCHOVIES; blanched BROCCOLI flowers with RED
PEPPERS — blend to a fine texture a handful of PARSLEY or
WATERCRESS with a few spoons of single CREAM, using a
blender or Magimix. Add to a vinaigrette, as above, or to a light
mayonnaise.

Wine vinaigrette   Mix 2 tablespoons each of: RED WINE,
OLIVE OIL, RED WINE VINEGAR, MILK or single CREAM.
Add SALT and PEPPER, 1 crushed GARLIC clove.

A dressing of OLIVE OIL and VINEGAR, SALT and PEPPER,
fresh TARRAGON leaves, warmed gently in a pan (this brings out
the taste and scent of the olive oil), then poured over just-steamed
vegetables such as ASPARAGUS or COURGETTES, will make a
simple and cleansing starter.

Memory of Mrs Sharp's eggs

Friends staying with us in Westchester were used to finding a box of
eggs on their dressing table, to be taken home Sunday evenings. The
eggs came from a farm nearby, a discovery for which I thank Tasha.
Each time we drove past those fields, Tasha, then four, asked to speak to
the cows. Her wish was granted, on the day that I felt gregarious. I drove
the car through the gates, knocked on the front door shaded by a
Mimosa tree, introduced myself and explained that my daughter was
longing to see the cows. Mrs Sharp, the owner, reacted immediately
with a welcome and took Tasha by the hand. Off we went. Cows, pigs,
sheep, hens and capons. We visited them all while Mrs Sharp and I
exchanged pieces of our lives. She had a house in Normandy where she
spent one or two summer months and where her cook came from, a
generation ago. Here, Mrs Sharp lived in two houses that stood only a
few feet apart. One was cool and light, called the Summer House,
without heating. In the late Fall, she moved to the Winter House for
warmth. She was a devout Catholic. One day we were given the
privilege of seeing her shrine of the Virgin Mary, secretly built in the
trunk of a pine tree. As we left, after the impromptu tour, Mrs Sharp
gave us a dozen eggs saying we could consider ourselves subscribers.
The system was simple: 'Drive up to the screen door in the back, any
time during the day, it is always open. In the hall there is a chest of
drawers on which stands a bowl full of eggs. Take a maximum of
twelve, sign the book, leave one dollar in the box.' The yolks were a

deep orange I have not seen since; a soft-boiled egg was a wonder. The hens' diet of grain and corn included scrapings and rinds of cheese picked up twice weekly from the local gourmet store.

Uova di Campania di Lino

BUTTER a gratin dish. Sprinkle with fresh BREADCRUMBS. Lay fine slices and strips of MOZZARELLA evenly over the breadcrumbs. Carefully break 2 EGGS per person over the cheese and gently cover with more mozzarella. Sprinkle generously with grated PARMESAN, a few more breadcrumbs, a few knobs of butter. Bake for 15 minutes in a hot oven.

Serve sprinkled generously with fresh parsley. Lino surveyed this last time, dribbled the dish with fresh OLIVE OIL, just a little LEMON JUICE, in fact drops, and an ANCHOVY over each egg. I had prepared RICE as an accompaniment, cooked with TURMERIC and SAFFRON, then fried with RED PEPPERS. This went well, as a bed for the eggs.

Poached Eggs Provençal

Should you have any bourride or fish stew left over, then poach the eggs directly in the BROTH or, if like me your poaching is messy, use an egg poacher, then transfer the perfectly shaped eggs to the broth when serving. Serve in a wide bowl with a few added VEGETABLES or sliced POTATOES, drop a spoon of AÏOLI or ROUILLE over the egg.

Otherwise, prepare a simple FISH STOCK. Add to the strained stock 1 LEEK per person, washed and chopped; 1 or 2 quartered TOMATOES, a strip of ORANGE PEEL, 1 clove of crushed GARLIC, a generous pinch of SAFFRON, 1 small POTATO per person, sliced and peeled. Simmer 10 minutes or until the potatoes are cooked. Remove the vegetables with a slotted spoon and keep warm.

Poach 1 EGG per person, place a few of the vegetables in each soup bowl, pour a ladleful of soup over the vegetables, sit the egg overall. Sprinkle with fresh PARSLEY and BASIL. A few CROÛTONS of fried bread on the side finish the meal.

Crème Caramel à la Grecque

I used to hate crème caramel. I looked suspiciously at the way it shook on my plate, a watery caramel puddle surrounding it. Years later, newly married, sailing in Greece on a beautiful and fairly comfortable sailing boat built for racing, Miles told me the best crème caramel he had ever eaten had been in Greece. And so it started. The first time I took up the challenge, Miles gave it six out of ten. Finally, I reached a score of nine. He still says the secret is to use sheep's milk. Here it is, more dense than the usual – it doesn't shake on the plate. This will feed eight people.

Butter a shallow, round glass dish, about 8in / 20cm in diameter. Melt 6oz / 150g of granulated white SUGAR in a small and heavy saucepan. As it turns to a deep tobacco colour, pour it into the glass dish, tipping it for even distribution. A trick: should the caramel go too far, almost burning, add 2 drops of a mild VINEGAR. This will stop the cooking immediately.

Beat 3 EGGS with 3 EGG YOLKS. Add 4oz / 100g WHITE SUGAR, 3 teaspoons of strong VANILLA ESSENCE, 3 teaspoons DARK RUM, pinch SALT. Pour in ½ pint / 300ml MILK and ½ pint / 300ml of single CREAM. Pour the mixture through a fine sieve over the caramel, by now hard.

Place the dish in a bain-marie of hot (not boiling) water. Bake for 1 hour until firm and barely wobbly. Testing with a silver knife, the blade should come out barely covered with the custard. Cool and chill. It will firm a little more.

When ready, loosen the edges with a blunt knife. Lay a serving dish on top, turn over, quickly. Each time I pray and each time it drops down neatly. Scrape bits of caramel from the bottom of the dish onto the dessert.

I serve the crème caramel with extra caramel. Melt another 6oz / 150g of white SUGAR; wait for it to turn translucent, then almost dark brown. Add the small drop of VINEGAR, wait for it to finish bubbling. Add a half teacupful of hot water, 3 or 4 tablespoons single CREAM. This can be done ahead of time and refrigerated. It will not harden.

Petits Suisses Dans Un Bain

This recipe, which I picked up years ago when we paid little attention to figure and health, is an adaptation of Richard Olney's Oeufs à la Suissesse.

Make a sauce béchamel, starting with a roux of 4 tablespoons BUTTER and 2 tablespoons FLOUR. Cook 2 or 3 minutes. Add, all at once, ½ pint / 300ml hot MILK, then SALT, freshly ground PEPPER and NUTMEG. When thick, remove from heat; add 4oz / 100g of freshly grated PARMESAN and 3 EGG YOLKS, stirring thoroughly and rapidly with a wooden spoon. Fold in 2 beaten EGG WHITES, gently and carefully.

Butter 6 or 8 individual soufflé pots or ramekins, depending on their size. Fill two thirds of the way up with the soufflé mixture. Poach in a pan of hot water in a slow oven until firm but spongy, 20 to 25 minutes. Unmould each ramekin, 1in / 2.5cm apart, onto a greased gratin dish. This can be done several hours ahead of time.

Sprinkle with freshly grated PARMESAN. Pour over the little soufflés enough hot single cream to immerse them by almost half. Place under a hot grill for 2 minutes, or in a hot oven for 5 to 6 minutes, until just browned and bubbling. Serve with a lot of freshly chopped PARSLEY and a few leaves of TARRAGON to cut the richness.

We don't have this often as it is very rich and the memory lasts for months, but there are cold days when it seems just perfect and delicious. Good as a starter, followed by little more than a slice of leftover roast meat and a salad.

White freesias and a red scarf; Olivia and Colin

As I walked into the kitchen this afternoon, I was struck by the small pot of flowers on the kitchen table. Maybe it was the light. It keeps happening. I had hardly noticed them in the morning. I walked around the table, examining all the angles. I wanted to put the flowers in my pocket, trap them between pages, something. And in a day or two, wilted, the flowers would lie in the rubbish. I stared into space for a while, then the food shopping on the counter brought my eye back into focus.

Olivia was coming to stay. I was looking forward to her presence. Last time, she brought white freesias and at night the cat slept with her. Olivia sat quietly at the table each morning, with a cup of coffee. She wore a silk dressing gown and read the newspaper; I crossed currents of air that held her scent as I moved around the house. Olivia is seventy, maybe seventy-three, the occasional trembling in her hands comes across as pretty.

I made an osso buco, having first read Elizabeth David and Marcella Hazan on the subject, prompted by Debby's enthusiasm for the dish which I had, so far, avoided trying. I prepared a more generous mirepoix than suggested and, too late, remembered that I only had fish stock left in the freezer. Anchovies are sometimes used with veal and I decided my stock would have to work, which it did, without making the dish taste fishy. The sauce was rich and gelatinous; I would make it the same way next time.

I made a bowl of long grain rice, tossed with the grated peel of many lemons, some olive oil and enough finely chopped parsley to fill two teacups to the brim. I would be happy, today, tomorrow and the next day, to eat just that rice with the taste of leaves and lemons. In fact, the next day, it became a salad for lunch, stretched with pieces of salami and black olives.

Food that week had a good rhythm. I froze what was left of the osso bucco sauce, to be used perhaps, with pasta. We had venison and sage sausages, cooked in red wine and mustard, and potato and leek soup. Two days later, I added the venison gravy to what was left of the soup for lunch with Colin. It tasted of mushroom for some reason I didn't bother to capture. Colin arrived wearing red scarf and tobacco-coloured corduroys, declaring he was on his way to see Dancing Ted, his haircutter in Kensington. I told him not to come back for at least two weeks afterwards. A day or two after that, lunch of saucisson chaud, pommes à l'huile, mustard, chives and parsley. That evening, I tossed bits of boudin into the remaining potatoes with a handful of loose corn and warmed it all quickly in a little more olive oil, just browning the edges of things.

Osso Buco with a Secret

I once used fish stock for this dish, faute de mieux, since it was all I had left in my freezer and there wasn't time to make a meat stock. The result was even better and not at all fishy. I now do this on purpose.

As to the meat: it is worth being fussy about the veal. Find a butcher who can supply fine, pale veal and who will cut the shank into slices at least 1–1¼in / 2.5–3cm thick. The best slices are from the middle of the shank, no more than 4in / 10cm across in diameter. Do not remove the outer membrane as this will hold the meat together.

For 6 you will need 9 OSSO BUCO pieces, unless they are quite large; 2 large, mild ONIONS; 2 medium CARROTS; 2 sticks CELERY; half a small FENNEL BULB; 3 cloves GARLIC, peeled and finely chopped; 1 strip of LEMON PEEL; ⁴/₅ pint / ½ litre FISH STOCK and ½ bottle of WHITE WINE; 14oz / 400g tin of whole TOMATOES; pinch SUGAR, ALLSPICE, GROUND FENNEL; 1 broken BAY LEAF; generous amount of freshly ground PEPPER, preferably coarse.

Finely chop the onions, carrot, celery and fennel. Sweat in a large frying pan, using a rich OLIVE OIL, for 10 to 15 minutes, over medium heat, stirring occasionally, letting the mirepoix stick just a little now and then. Add the garlic and lemon peel, stir for 2 minutes and transfer to the bottom of a large oven dish, preferably enamelled cast iron (I use Le Creuset) with a tight fitting lid and no more than 3in/7.5cm deep.

Dust the veal very lightly with flour and brown the meat in the same frying pan as for the mirepoix. Add more oil if necessary – over medium heat. Fry the veal in batches, about 3 minutes on each side, until lightly browned. Transfer each batch as you go along to the oven dish, one piece leaning against the other so that the marrow in the centre of the bone doesn't spill out into the sauce.

Pour out any excess burnt fat from the frying pan and return it to medium heat. Pour in half a bottle of good white wine (I use Sancerre) and scrape up the burnt solids on the bottom. Boil for a minute, then lower the heat; add the fish stock and tin of tomatoes, roughly breaking them up. Stir in the sugar and spices, bay leaf and ground pepper. Simmer for 2 minutes and pour over the veal. Cover the dish and bake in a not quite medium oven for an hour. Turn the meat over each half hour and baste.

The osso buco will be ready in another 40 minutes but will taste even better tomorrow, in which case remove from oven after the first hour and cool, then refrigerate.

Reheat in a medium hot oven for an hour, covered. Baste and turn the meat again each half hour. Leave to rest in the turned off oven, door ajar or, if using a heavy cast iron dish, leave on the counter for fifteen minutes.

There is a tradition of serving osso buco with a mixture of grated lemon peel and parsley, which can be somewhat over-powering rather than complementary. I prefer to have a LEMONY RICE on the side.

A Lemony Rice

Grate the peel of 3 LEMONS, using the larger holes of the grater. Finely chop enough PARSLEY to fill 2 teacups to the brim – this means buying a bunch of parsley the size of a head of lettuce. Combine the lemon and parsley; set aside. It will remain fresh, covered in the fridge for a couple of hours.

I use Uncle Ben's rice, not quite doubling the quantity of water. This recipe being for 6–8 people, I use 4 teacupsful of rice (mounded) to 6½ teacupsful of water. Bring the water to the boil, using a heavy saucepan with tight fitting lid. As the water reaches a boil, put in a pinch of SALT and a good pinch of SAFFRON strands. Stir in the rice, lower the heat and cover. Simmer 5 minutes. Turn off the heat; do not disturb for 20 minutes. The rice should be perfect.

Stir in OLIVE OIL, enough to just coat the grains and keep them separate, then coarsely ground PEPPER. Add half the lemon and parsley mixture, turn into a serving bowl, cover with foil or a lid and keep warm until ready to serve (it will remain just right for at least half an hour in a barely warm oven). Just before serving, toss in the remaining parsley and lemon peel and grate a little fresh PARMESAN over the top.

November

... he drew a quick picture of the kitchen, including the ladder hung horizontally from the ceiling...

Branko comes for dinner; Toby is in love; Colin draws over the line; a picnic

Branko called. His book was almost finished. We went to a lecture at the ICA given by the French philosopher, Jacques Derrida. We returned to my house for dinner and Branko, in his rolling accent, a mixture of Yugoslav and Italian, told me the only thing a refugee may keep, in exile, is his accent.

We sat down to the meal I had prepared earlier. Cumberland sausages, browned and then simmered for twenty minutes in red wine, mustard, soy and a touch of vinegar. The sauce becomes dark and sticky. I used to do this in America with Italian sausages, both sweet and hot, spiced with fennel, but so far have not seen these in London. We had a paillasson de pommes de terre – potatoes peeled and grated, squeezed dry in a kitchen towel, then cooked, flattened like a pancake, in a well-oiled and buttered cast-iron pan. At the end, it looks like a straw mat on the doorstep. Hence its name, more appealing in French. Then red cabbage, stewed with apples and caraway seeds.

Toby called to tell me he was in love: 'A raven-haired beauty, in the middle of a divorce, fending off a demented husband. Will you be our drop for exchanging billets doux in large manilla envelopes?' I ignored the obvious, hoped his dreams would come true, and said yes.

It was time to christen our new address and I invited about thirty people to an evening picnic. Open house from six to midnight. I was preparing a chickpea salad with burnt almonds and cuttlefish. Dougie, the electrician, arrived to fix the ceiling spotlights in the kitchen. He found himself hanging the new curtains in the sitting room and making mayonnaise. I gave him a taste but he thought it was quite peculiar. With my right arm stiff with the effort of beating, I asked him to take over. He finished the mayonnaise as I dribbled the olive oil into the bowl. He said it was more fun to wire a house. I sat him down with a cup of tea and gave him a taste of the chickpeas. Those were more to his liking. I turned to the lentils. I was going to mix them with pieces of smoked duck and a large quantity of finely chopped parsley, mint and spring onions, as though for a tabbouleh salad. Two days after the party, I turned this into lentil soup, adding wine and stock and cream. The fresh mint gave it a sorrel-like taste. There still being some jambon de Bayonne and pâté left over, the children and I continued the feast. Colin dropped in on the right day and shared a little more with us. While at table, he drew a quick picture of the kitchen, including the ladder hung horizontally from the ceiling. Carefully, he drew the pots and baskets and plait of garlic that hung from each of the ladder's steps. I looked at the semi-architectural drawing when he had finished. I admired the gentle, almost Victorian sketch. My eye travelled along it up to the staircase, and there, at the top, was a woman, wearing boots, shielding a breast with a large hat. Nothing else. 'Colin! Who is that?' 'A running fantasy,' he answered, helping himself to more pâté and chickpeas.

Salade de Courgettes et Tomates

The only difficulty, if this is to be perfect, is to find really young and small courgettes and translucent, fruit-like tomatoes.

Cut the COURGETTES into ½in / 1.25cm thick rounds, unpeeled. Blanch in salted, boiling water for just 1–2 minutes. Drain and dry carefully. Arrange on a plate with the sliced TOMATOES. Warm gently a dressing of HAZELNUT OIL, LEMON JUICE and a little mild SHERRY VINEGAR. Pour this over the vegetables. Sprinkle a generous quantity of PARSLEY and CHIVES, a couple of handfuls or more. Season with SALT and freshly ground PEPPER; mix in Niçoise BLACK OLIVES and, if you have it, slices of a good SALAMI to suit your eye and taste. Perhaps fresh sardines, quickly grilled. A simple and easy lunch.

If the vegetables are not perfect, bake in a gratin dish, with the oil and seasoning, for 30 minutes to an hour, until well caramelised. Cool, then add a dash of VINEGAR.

Chickpeas and Chickpeas and Chickpeas

I use these, and other dried beans, throughout the year – hot, cold, for salads, soups. I never tire of them. Economical, lasting and versatile.

My basic system is to soak the CHICKPEAS in cold water to cover for several hours. Drain, cover with fresh water or, preferably, a strong CHICKEN STOCK. Bring slowly to a simmer, covered. They are cooked in about 2 hours (depending on variety and age), to my taste, which means still quite firm, a little like a cashew nut. Another hour or so will soften them further if you prefer them less firm.

Since I usually cook them in a strong stock, I don't use wine or many strong seasonings. I like GROUND CUMIN, a BAY LEAF, sometimes GARLIC and GINGER, a muslin bag of BOUQUET GARNI. The stock eliminates the need for salt. Once cooked, coated with the stock that has reduced to a syrup consistency, add HAZELNUT OIL (adding to the nut-like taste), a mild SHERRY VINEGAR, slivers of ONION, LEMON JUICE, a few WALNUTS, or ALMONDS lightly toasted to bring out their taste. Toss while still warm, but the chickpeas will continue to absorb and an hour later will need a little more of everything.

Variations: chopped ANCHOVIES, GREEN OLIVES, chopped raw, sweet RED PEPPER, a little CREAM in the dressing which distributes the taste of anchovy throughout.

CUTTLEFISH OR SQUID, bottled – I use the brand Medusa, a useful last-minute addition for unexpected guests – fresh CORIANDER and MINT.

Chopped TOMATOES, PARSLEY and MINT in truly lavish quantities, finely chopped, as though for a tabbouleh salad; AÏOLI on the side.

SAFFRON, warmed in OLIVE OIL; flower heads of BROCCOLI.

English Sausages à la Française

This is a way of treating English sausages to a French bath in wine, as though saucissons de Toulouse. I use a combination of VENISON SAUSAGES, with CUMBERLAND or SAGE SAUSAGES, a home-made mixture from a reliable and caring butcher. Cooked this way, then cooled and sliced, they taste like small pâtés; people are disconcerted, not quite certain what they are. The sausages can of course be eaten hot, sliced, lightly covered with the cooking liquor.

Bring to a simmer 3 parts RED WINE to 1 part water, enough to just cover the sausages in a deep saucepan. They will float just below the surface. Other than a teaspoon of VINEGAR, seasoning isn't really necessary. The sausages are strong and their scent will permeate the wine and water.

When the liquor reaches a boil, turn down to a simmer, prick the sausages lightly with a fork and slide into the saucepan. Maintain a gentle simmer and cook, uncovered, for 20 minutes. Turn off the heat; leave to cool.

Remove the sausages and refrigerate for a couple of hours or more. This is necessary for them to be firm enough to slice neatly. Slice the sausages on the bias, forming longish ovals about a 1/4in / 6mm thick. Arrange on a dish alternating each variety, contrasting dark venison meat with the paler Cumberland or sage variety. They are delicious with almost any kind of VEGETABLE SALAD or tossed with tiny NEW POTATOES dressed in OLIVE OIL and MUSTARD.

The wine and water turn into a valuable STOCK. I used some of this the other day to cook BLACK BEANS. The stock gave the beans a deep, rich, meaty taste. After 2 hours, they were just tender. I blended them roughly, laid the purée in an oiled gratin dish, sprinkled a little more WINE and OIL over the top, then grated GRUYÈRE and PARMESAN over the beans and baked the dish in a hot oven for 15 minutes. I served the beans with a ring of TOMATO SAUCE around each helping. The next day, I used four tablespoons of the puréed beans for a tomato sauce to which I added 2 cups of leftover BOLOGNESE SAUCE. We had this over a plain dish of RICE coloured with TURMERIC.

Sausages pour Branko

This should also be known as pour Tony. I gather this has become a favourite of his. It can be prepared ahead of time, reheated gently for a few minutes before serving. Only use sausages made by a reliable and inspired butcher, sons serving at the counter, wife by the cash register. I find one type of sausage too much of one thing; having two or three varying tastes creates a pleasing balance. For a combination of 3 venison sausages, 2 Cumberland, 2 or 3 spicy or hot ones – enough for four people.

Brown the SAUSAGES well and evenly for 10 minutes, in a heavy cast-iron pan. Scrape up the solids with RED WINE, 2 glasses thickened with a heaped tablespoon of strong DIJON MUSTARD and one of TOMATO PURÉE, a glass of leftover GRAVY or a shot of SOY, a touch of VINEGAR and PORT, ½ teaspoon of ALLSPICE and CHINESE FIVE SPICES. Simmer half an hour, turning the sausages occasionally in the sauce. It will become rich and dark. Correct the balance of thickness with more red wine if necessary. Salt will not be needed.

Serve each person with a selection of sausages and a more than decorative amount of chopped PARSLEY to balance the richness of the sauce.

Un Paillasson de Pommes de Terre

This is named for its resemblance to a straw mat by the front door . . . simple and good.

Grate 1 large, peeled POTATO per person. Put the grated potatoes into a bowl of cold water to cover, with a couple of tablespoons of VINEGAR to prevent them from changing colour. Leave for an hour or so to unstarch.

Drain and heap into a tea towel. Roll the tea towel into a sausage, twist the ends and squeeze out thoroughly all the wetness from the potatoes. Transfer to a cast iron pan, heated just below burning point with BUTTER and PEANUT OIL. Pack down the grated potatoes, season with SALT and freshly ground PEPPER, turn the heat down to low. Cook for 20 minutes, uncovered, without disturbing. You can leave the paillasson at this point, and continue when you are almost ready for dinner.

With a spatula, loosen the paillasson from the sides and bottom of the pan, and quickly turn it over onto a platter. Put fresh butter and oil into the skillet, heat until it sizzles once again, return the paillasson, uncooked side down. Repeat as before.

Slice an ONION into airmail paper-thin slivers, mix with freshly chopped PARSLEY, SALT and PEPPER. Sprinkle over the paillasson when serving.

Chou Rouge aux Pommes

This should be prepared a day ahead of time. It gets better and better. For four people melt about 6oz/150g fresh pieces of UNSMOKED BACON or BEEF SUET, in a large pan. To the melted fat, add ½ teaspoon each of CARAWAY SEEDS and ALLSPICE, a dozen crushed JUNIPER BERRIES, a few PEPPERCORNS. Toss for a minute to release the scent. Add 2 tart APPLES, such as Granny Smiths, peeled, cored and quartered. Cook until roughly puréed. Lower the heat, add a medium head of RED CABBAGE, cut into thin strips. Mix well with the apples and spices, pour in enough CHICKEN STOCK to almost cover the cabbage (or STOCK from a SAUCISSON DE TOULOUSE) and 3 tablespoons of CIDER VINEGAR. Add SALT to your taste, cover and simmer gently for about 1 hour, stirring occasionally to check the cabbage is moist.

Remove the lid, simmer until the cabbage stews to a slightly sticky and caramelised consistency. Check the balance of tartness; it may need another tablespoon of vinegar, perhaps a dash of brown SUGAR.

Serve with a roast of pork; equally with derivatives – sausages or beans with pieces of bacon or pancetta.

Stephan; forgetting the pheasants

Stephan came for tea on a Sunday, with Stephanie, their children Larissa and Alexander, and a brace of pheasant, unplucked, undrawn. A charming and awkward treat, of great interest to the cats – we looked for a safe place to hang the birds, out of feline reach. Someone produced a nail which Stephan hammered above the kitchen door, outside. There they remained for three days, four days, five days, as I thought of the last time Stephan had brought a brace, taking me back, once again, to Westchester. There it had been easy. I plucked them outside on the deck, feathers flew in all directions, no one minded, there was time, space and peace of mind. Later, Miles drew them and the next day we sat down to a rare meal in America.

But now, in London, in an unfinished house, my senses and energies scattered in too many directions, the sight of those birds outside the door reduced me to a state of nervous tension. By the sixth day, they became a permanent fixture I almost managed to ignore were it not for the cats sitting underneath, gazing up, tails rigid with concentration. Was Stephan an old enough, close enough friend, to understand my lack of enterprise and gratitude?

Stephan is godfather to Tasha. His inner eye sees magic in places where other people see only what they see. I expect him to share his sight with his goddaughter some day, along with his culinary skills. Thinking of this, on the seventh day of the pheasants, by now steaming in the November chill, I plucked out two long feathers as a souvenir and threw out the bodies, hoping Stephan's tendency to romance would include absolution. I bought two breasts of duck for the children and I stuck the feathers on top. I interpreted Debby's recipe, via Michel Guérard. Chrissie called and thought of her reminded me of the way she roasts potatoes. Feeling peaceful as always after talking to Chrissie, I sat down to a good meal.

Magrets de Canard à la Debby

This is rich to the palate, depleting to the budget, but twice a year is enough; the memory will last for months. Recipes are a game of plagiary. This is no exception – starting with Michel Guérard, then Debby, who urged me to try it, as I did, in my own way.

Duck meat is rich, the breast may weigh up to 12oz / 350g, but I allow 3 breasts for 4 people, just in case one of us is particularly greedy that night. The children and I shared a pair and the next day there was enough for them to take to school in their packed lunch boxes, to the delight of their friends.

Score the skin of the DUCK BREASTS two or three times, in a pleasing pattern. Brown the breasts at near-burning heat in PEANUT OIL, about 3 minutes on each side, then 1 extra minute with the lid on the frying pan, for a strong pink; otherwise, 2 more minutes. Reduce the cooking time if the size of the duck breasts you have bought is smaller than the ones I describe, or less than 1½in / 3.75cm thick in the middle. Remove to a warm oven where they will finish cooking gently, without overcooking. You can keep them waiting up to 15 minutes.

Discard the burnt fat from the pan, add a knob of BUTTER, melt 1 level tablespoon CASTER SUGAR with 1 tablespoon good SHERRY or TARRAGON VINEGAR. As this turns to caramel, deglaze the pan further with a glass of WHITE WINE, or at least 8 tablespoons. Add 3 tablespoons of ARMAGNAC or MADEIRA (which I prefer). Reduce the heat after 1 minute, add a 10oz / 275g pot of DOUBLE CREAM, simmer gently, reducing to the consistency of single cream. Add a small tin or jar of GREEN PEPPERCORNS, with their juice, or only half the peppercorns if you prefer less spice. Stir in 3 tablespoons of STOCK if available, or GRAVY, otherwise just a little water and a dash of WORCES-TERSHIRE SAUCE, then 2 tablespoons of TAWNY PORT. Pour over the duck breasts and serve, slicing the meat on the bias and very thin.

I serve this with Chrissie's POTATOES (see below), leaving just enough room to gasp down a salad. Or, STRING BEANS and grilled TOMATOES.

Chrissie's Potatoes

These are now everybody's potatoes. The method has been passed on to all friends as each time they help themselves to more, asking for the recipe.

Use large, not very waxy POTATOES. Peel and cut into sizes a little bigger than a bite. They will shrink during the cooking. Parboil the potatoes for 5 to 10 minutes, until just softening on the outside. Drain, return to the saucepan and, lid tightly on, shake in all directions. You will end up with potatoes looking like balls of fluff, as Debby puts it.

On the stove, warm a ½in / 1.25cm of OIL and BUTTER in a shallow gratin dish large enough to hold your quantity of potatoes without crowding. When the fat is hot, put in the potatoes; as they sizzle, transfer to the top of a hot oven. After half an hour, turn the potatoes over, bake for another 30–40 minutes. They can wait for another 10 minutes, oven turned off. They will have crisped perfectly on the outside. Crunchy, little bits clinging to the sides, melting inside. Serve sprinkled with SALT and freshly ground PEPPER, chopped PARSLEY.

Dinner at Elizabeth's, a mystery guest

Went to Elizabeth's house for dinner. The round table was laid for nine. One seat remained empty and Elizabeth told us the surprise guest would turn up for pudding, but the doorbell rang before we finished the second course. I recognized Miles' voice at the door. Ian, on my left, leapt up to his feet to embrace his oldest friend with his usual Latin exuberance. Miles, more Anglo-Saxon in this respect, fended him off like a woman who keeps saying no when she means yes. It was touching and I waited for the pudding thinking about surprises, attacked by a bout of philosophy. Affection outlives passion and argument. Before I became completely immersed, a chocolate biscuit appeared on the table. The recipe follows, with the lady's permission. Good, simple to make, rich, and I would never think of producing such a demanding weight to the palate after a full meal, but it is a recipe worth having for the right day, preferably of a cold month, which this was.

Elizabeth's Broken Biscuit Chocolate Cake

This is rich, delicious and a little goes far. This quantity is enough for 6 people. Serving it with cream is unnecessary but it gives the illusion of balance and 'cuts' one 'richesse' with another. Elizabeth's source is *English Country House Cooking* by Fortune Stanley and is, I gather, almost faithful to it. My addition is to mix double cream with a tablespoon or two of dark rum, a dash of vanilla essence, lemon juice or a grating of orange peel, and to serve this as an accompaniment.

10oz / 250g broken Petit Beurre Lu BISCUITS; 5oz / 120g CASTER SUGAR; 5oz / 120g BUTTER (I use salted); 7½oz / 190g best DARK CHOCOLATE; 1 EGG, lightly beaten; 1 tablespoon strong, dark, expresso COFFEE; 2oz / 60g chopped WALNUTS.

Cream the butter and sugar, mix with the broken biscuits (crush them gently with a rolling pin). Add 5oz / 120g of the chocolate, grated, then the beaten egg, coffee and walnuts. Pour the mixture into a buttered soufflé dish and leave to harden overnight in the refrigerator.

Loosen the edges with a blunt knife and turn out onto a serving dish. Sprinkle with the remaining chocolate, grated.

December

... I noticed the cast iron pot
was cracked with rust...

Norfolk; an old friend; Christmas with the plumber

Went up to Norfolk, a little nervously, for a weekend with an old friend from another context and different days. We spent the first night in a hotel in Bury St Edmunds, on our way up to the North Sea. We were shown to a bedroom down a long, winding hall, up three steps, down two steps, white walls, red carpet; more red carpet. And in the room, a huge, four-poster bed. 'Was a St Edmund buried here?' I asked as I drew a bath, feeling young, old, shy; bumping into my own arms and legs.

We continued our journey early next morning. Churches like small boxes at every bend, pebbled houses, holm oaks, occasionally a grand house rising in the middle of unspoiled and farmed land; we drove past a scarecrow and thought it was a man, running away – empty legs flapped in the wind; past a disused railway station with a name that triggered a vision of city and crowd on the deserted platform; we stopped for a late lunch in Ely, in a restaurant by the cathedral, The Old Firehouse. Our elbows rested on a white linen tablecloth. Lace and holes were neatly ironed over with starch. Middle-aged ladies served us good English food without fuss. Roast saddle of lamb. A little port in the gravy. Perfectly simple. I declined the mint sauce and redcurrant jelly, although well prepared: I think of them as confiture avec la viande. We raised our glasses to unanswered questions and felt safer the next day after a walk on the beach. Open space and a sea that was indeed 'mucous-coloured and scrotum tightening'. We were back on familiar territory, arguing about why I still hadn't read *Ulysses*. Who knows, I thought during the drive back to London, the answer to anything for more than a day. This old friend was Miles.

Christmas was just a few weeks away. Time yet to make the pudding but this was an unnecessary reflex since none of us were planning to be home this year. In America, most years, saddle of lamb was the Christmas lunch as the taste of Thanksgiving turkey still lingered a month later. Miles introduced me to that special cut of meat, explaining that the difference in texture was because of the carving along the grain. Respecting the delicacy, I kept the gravy light, almost thin. I coated the saddle with breadcrumbs, mustard and parsley, then roasted the meat at high heat leaving it to rest afterwards for at least twenty minutes. On

the side, instead of confiture, a confit d'oignons, and once again the
family favourite of pommes sautées.

I smile at the memory of our first Christmas at Pea Pond House. A
small white van appeared at the back door. We were in the middle of
lunch. In walked the plumber, with wife, two children and small gifts, to
pay respect. Pinching ourselves, we sat them down, wondering whether
this was custom or tradition and should we offer what was left of the
main course. And a month later they moved to Florida.

Saddle of Lamb, Just a Little Piquante

This is a most delicate cut of meat – weighing about 5½ pounds,
more or less 2½ kilos, unless you buy the whole saddle which
includes the 'chump end', but, as that part of the saddle rises into
a hump, this makes even cooking throughout impossible, I ask
the butcher to cut the saddle at that point. This limits you to 6
people (almost half the weight is bone) but, being an expensive
cut of meat, it is just as well. Anyway, appreciation lessens with
the number of people. The butcher should remove the skin and
secure the overhanging flaps neatly under the saddle with needle
and string. At home, I trim the fat on top of the saddle even more,
leaving only a thin film, nearly revealing the red colour of meat
beneath it. If you ask the butcher to do this for you, he will
intimidate you by saying you need all that fat for protection –
which is nonsense and ruins the gravy.

Oil lightly the bottom of a heavy oven dish, cast-iron and fairly
shallow by preference, just large enough to hold the SADDLE and
gravy. I use, for once, an almost tasteless oil such as PEANUT OIL.
Break up 2 thick slices of white BREAD, including crust, and
crumble in the blender. Melt a few tablespoons of salted BUTTER
with two pinches of FENNEL SEEDS. Mix into the breadcrumbs.

Spread thickly with Dijon or Amora MUSTARD, the top and
sides of the saddle (or, for a change, the grainy moutarde à
l'ancienne). You will need most of a small pot. Using your
fingers, cover the mustard base with pinches of the buttered
breadcrumbs, patting them into place over the saddle. The
mustard base will act as a holding agent for the breadcrumbs.
Sprinkle chopped, fresh ROSEMARY (must be fresh) over and
around the saddle.

Make a paste of a tablespoon each of TOMATO PURÉE, ANCHOVY PASTE and MUSTARD. Dilute with two capfuls of Gordon's GIN (stronger taste of juniper), a dash each of TABASCO and WORCESTERSHIRE SAUCE, then a small glass of MADEIRA and a more generous glass of RED WINE. Pour this around the meat.

Have ready on the stove a small saucepan of four ladlefuis of STOCK simmering with a glass of RED WINE and any leftover gravy you may have. I keep 1 or 2 small jars in the freezer to which I add whatever is left of any gravy, even if it is only a few tablespoons.

Heat the oven to a high temperature. Roast the meat for about 30 minutes, turn off the oven and, with door ajar, leave the meat to rest another 10 minutes. This relaxes the muscle, so the meat is more tender and allows it to finish, gently, its cooking. During the half hour of cooking, baste the meat once, spooning the gravy over the breadcrumbs to brown and crust, then scrape the sides of the dish which will be caramelising and distribute back into the sauce, adding, as it reduces, more liquid from the saucepan on top of the stove. At the end of the half hour, transfer the sauce that is in the oven dish back to the saucepan on your stove, simmer and check for seasoning. A little more MUSTARD and a dash of SINGLE CREAM are usually a good idea.

The carving is crucial and delicate. The saddle must be carved lengthwise, along the backbone and along the grain of the meat; fairly thin slices, about ¼in / 6mm thick. Cutting along the grain completely changes the texture of what would otherwise be a lamb chop. Serve the long slices with a piece of the mustard crust, by now quite scrunchy and just a little sharp from the mustard.

The cooking time is only a guide. Ovens can be so temperamental, different in each house. I purposely avoid giving a temperature – just roast the saddle at a higher heat than you do for the usual roast chicken or beef, but not high enough to turn roasting into singeing.

I usually serve the saddle with pommes sautées and, instead of redcurrant jelly, a confit d'oignons. More vegetables than that are, to me, confusing to the palate, except for a salad later.

Confit d'Oignons

Perhaps a little rudely, I refer to the idea of redcurrant jelly with meats as confiture avec la viande. To me, a confit d'oignons is a much more interesting and subtle companion. Cooked in the following way, the onions seem almost candied and melt in the mouth. I like them cold if any are leftover, or 1 tablespoon spread over an omelette just before folding and turning onto a plate. My addition of a red pepper is optional, but I think it gives a balance to the taste. It is best prepared a day or two ahead of time, gently re-heated in five minutes. As it needs a constant eye during the last half hour, I cook it in the evening while preparing dinner and can stir whenever necessary as I lay the table and prepare our meal for that evening.

For six you will need 1 large RED PEPPER, cut lengthwise, seeded and ribbed, thinly sliced, and 5 large ONIONS (over 3lbs / 1.3kg in total weight), thinly sliced. Melt a heaped table-spoon BUTTER with 3 tablespoons good OLIVE OIL in a large frying pan, at medium heat. As the butter sizzles, toss in the sliced pepper, cover, cook 5 minutes to wilt the pepper. It will just start to burn here and there.

As the pepper cooks, start to slice the onions. Uncover the peppers after 5 minutes, scrape up the browned bits of the pan with a metal spatula, add another tablespoon of butter and three more tablespoons of olive oil. Toss in the onions in batches, each time turning over those at the bottom of the pan that have started to wilt, mixing in the new batch with the old. When all the onions are in, cover and leave on a medium flame for 20 minutes. By now, you will be in floods of tears and need a moment to clear your eyes from the sting of all those onions.

Uncover the pan. The level of onions will have dropped by half and they will have started to brown and stick to the pan. Scrape up well those on the bottom, using the metal spatula, and toss the onions distributing the caramelised bits and using the onion liquid to deglaze the pan with. Cover again and leave another 10 minutes. Uncover and repeat as above. Lower the flame to low and leave, covered, another 10 minutes.

Uncover for the last time. The onions will now be sitting in a small amount of brown liquor. Transfer to a smaller pan, for

onions cooking in a mound can do so for longer without burning
than if they are spread out thinly. I start with a frying pan
measuring 12in / 30cm in diameter, then down to an 8in / 20cm
cast-iron frying pan – the heavier the better, in order to control
the burning. Cook over a low flame, 15 to 20 minutes or until the
liquid has disappeared and the onions start to stick again.

Scrape and stir, adding another tablespoon of butter. Keep
stirring and scraping gently and quite often, and cook another 30
to 45 minutes. Cool and keep in the refrigerator.

To re-heat, I use an even smaller pan, about 6in / 15cm across.
Densely packed, the onions will re-heat without burning. They
will have become dark and caramelised with an almost jam-like
consistency. I only add SALT and PEPPER at the end. Their
sweetness varies and only at the end do you know which way the
onions have developed, but don't forget to season them. Serve 2
heaped tablespoons onto each plate, shaped into a little mound.

Pommes Sautées

A family favourite in any house, here or in France, with many
variations. Mine: for four people.

Peel and cube 6 large, not too floury POTATOES into
1/2–3/4 in/ 1.25–1.85cm pieces. Warm a pan large enough to
hold the potatoes only just a little crowded, with enough OLIVE
OIL (or GOOSE FAT or BACON FAT) to cover the bottom of the
pan. Put in the cubed potatoes, toss 1 medium ONION, finely
chopped over the top, cover the pan and leave over a medium
heat for 5 minutes. The steam from the moisture in the onions
and potatoes will soften the potatoes evenly.

Uncover, use a spatula to scrape up the potatoes roughly, toss
and turn mixing the browned bits. Do this roughly on purpose –
little bits will break off the potatoes and form little crusts. Leave
on a medium to low flame, uncovered, for another 20–30
minutes. As more crusts form on the bottom of the pan, scrape up
and toss, repeating this several times. As the potatoes shrink and
brown, the bottom of the pan may dry. Add knobs of butter, or
goose or bacon fat – whichever you have chosen.

After 10 minutes, add SALT, PEPPER and 3 cloves of
GARLIC, cut in half (I use big pieces as I like the surprise of a bite

of browned garlic but, if you don't, chop the garlic more finely
than I do). Add chopped, fresh ROSEMARY if you have it (leaves
from at least three branches), during the last 5 minutes, just
enough time to distribute the oils. Longer than that, they will die.
At the last minute, just before serving, add lots of chopped
PARSLEY and SPRING ONIONS, tossing and turning with the
spatula (never a wooden spoon).

Variations: Add during the last ten minutes 6 or 7 chopped
ANCHOVY FILLETS and / or finely sliced and chopped RED
PEPPERS; a thick slice of PANCETTA or PROSCIUTTO,
chopped.

Lino comes to London; a boxer's cure

Lino was in London for three days, free at last to travel, passport and
reputation restored. He was even larger than before. Surely prison food
should have affected his waistline otherwise? He still reminded me of
Marcello Mastroianni; if only he would lose forty pounds. He laughed
and said that in prison, cooking became a consuming and meticulous
pastime. The cell had a camping-style burner, two pots and one frying
pan. No knives. They chopped onions with the lid of an opened tin and
crushed garlic by rolling the body of the same tin over it. They were only
allowed out once a day for a fifteen minute stretch in the yard. A
transitory cell was more restricted than a permanent cell, and far less
'comfortable', he said. The planning of a meal was meticulous and
prolonged – a military campaign.

The children were as pleased to see him as I was and Georgia, who
had twisted her knee, was given full attention. Lino examined her injury
with professional comments and, telling me of a boxer friend of his,
opened up the kitchen cupboards to find the necessary ingredients for a
cure: bowl and wooden spoon, two handfuls of flour, two tablespoons
of olive oil, of course; the white of an egg, two shots of Aquavit. This
thick paste was gently spread over Georgia's knee, which was then
wrapped in three tea towels. She went to bed in the important
wrapping. She rose the next morning, if not miraculously cured,
certainly with the swelling impressively reduced and the pain gone.

Once again, we discussed plans for another year during dinner. Lino
was going to Africa but we would see him again in the spring. He ate
well now that his digestion was at rest. I gave him a boeuf Miroton, then

a winter's compote de fruits, a favourite of Tasha's. I would be going to New York in February, I told him. 'Home?' asked Lino. 'No, this is home' I answered. 'Bene, bene' said Lino approvingly.

Boeuf Miroton

This leftover dish was added to my repertory during a week in January years ago, when my father came to stay in Beaver Dam. Thirteen inches of snow had fallen that week, and for thirty six hours we were cut off. Miles came home that first evening on foot, having left the car at the end of the driveway, three quarters of a mile away from the house. He had impulsively bought in New York a beautiful piece of roast rib of beef. He found himself walking the driveway, snow up to his knees, parcel of meat in one hand, briefcase in the other, his smart brown hat the only protection against the elements. He was an incongruous sight, but pleased with himself.

Miles presented the precious parcel to my father, who within seconds neatly 'wasted' it by removing the bones in one swift slice of a sharp knife, leaving a far less impressive piece of meat. Miles stood by, still dripping snow, a little deflated, as my father explained that all would be put to use. The bones were baked at a high heat, then turned into a pot with wine and water and herbs for a rich stock which then turned into a wonderful gravy, in which my father had blended, at the last minute, a small handful of fresh mint, something he usually does with lamb, but that day decided to try with beef. Two days later, still snowbound, the leftover beef became a new meal.

The miroton sauce is a centuries-old classic revamping for beef, which I apply to other meats now: lamb, veal or pork. Pre-heat the oven to medium hot. Arrange slices of leftover BEEF or LAMB on a heat-proof platter or shallow, copper sauté pan. Cook in BUTTER and OLIVE OIL, 1 large ONION and 1 CARROT per two people, finely chopped. When softened and lightly browned, add 1 tablespoon good VINEGAR for two, cover with STOCK or leftover GRAVY, then a glass of RED WINE, TOMATO PURÉE and DIJON MUSTARD thickening the wine, a little finely chopped GARLIC. Cover and simmer 40 minutes, checking the level of liquid and adjusting, if necessary, with more wine or stock.

Add small CAPERS (*not* the large ones) and chopped GREEN
OLIVES to your taste; pour the sauce around and over the meat.
Lay a ribbon of fresh, chopped PARSLEY and freshly made white
BREADCRUMBS over the meat. Pour melted BUTTER over that,
cover with foil and bake just long enough to heat, 5–10 minutes.
Remove the foil during the last 3 or 4 minutes to brown the
breadcrumbs.

A *Winter's Compote de Fruits*

This is a favourite of Tasha's, easy to do, extremely nutritious,
not very elegant. But I agree with her, in dead of winter it is
comforting and good. A few fresh mint leaves, if you can find
them at that time of year in your garden, failing that, a scattering
of grapes, lifts its appearance.

For four: Combine in a bowl ¼lb / 110g each of DRIED
FIGS, preferably Turkish; APRICOTS, unsweetened; PRUNES,
unpitted; APPLE RINGS; SULTANAS. Just cover with half a
bottle of semi-sweet WHITE WINE. Soak for a few hours.
Transfer the fruit and wine to a saucepan, add 4 to 5 tablespoons
of caster SUGAR, a strip of LEMON RIND, dash of LEMON
JUICE, ¼ teaspoon each of NUTMEG, CINNAMON, ALL-
SPICE, CLOVES.

Simmer gently for 45 minutes to one hour, adding wine if
necessary. The level of liquid should be maintained half way up
the fruit. Add 2 tablespoons of BRANDY during the last 10
minutes of cooking. Cool. Sprinkle 2 tablespoons of ROSE-
WATER over the fruit. Serve with cream or a Sabayon sauce (see
page 6).

Truffles in Pimlico; steak and kidney in Bedford

Stephan called. It was time for our more or less monthly lunch. 'Same
time, same place – the white truffles have arrived,' was his spoken
invitation: one o'clock in Pimlico. Once again, the owner of the
restaurant marched up to our table; once again, I imagined him in a suit
of lights, but he would never be a bullfighter: he was a six-inches-too-
tall Italian who snapped his fingers and clapped both hands at his
waiters. Last year, the weekly shipment of white truffles arrived just

after our lunch, in a white container the size of a picnic hamper, carefully sealed and tied with wire. Scent escaped nevertheless, and within a minute, was almost overpowering. By the time the Signore had opened the container, in front of us and removed small parcels of truffles wrapped in thick, white linen cloths, I appreciated what he had told us about the smell causing a combination of hallucination and giddiness. The sensation helped him to ignore his numb hands after two or three hours of washing the truffles under freezing cold water.

Now, Stephan ordered our meal, after the formality of greeting and a joke about the priorities in life, in fluent Italian. Bresaola to start with, a dressing of olive oil scented with a truffle; plain risotto with at least half a truffle grated over the rice. 'Grouse,' Stephan said, 'the English just don't know how to eat them. I suppose they can't know everything,' he added, with admiring emphasis on the last word. 'I told my butcher, the other day, that I wanted grouse dead but fresh. Grouse is *born* gamy, it doesn't need to be hung. The man was unenthusiastic but he cheered up when I told him forty people were coming to dinner: we made an amicable deal on the price. Went home, late, wondered what now. Put the grouse in a roasting pan, a very big one, covered the birds with green bacon, stuffed them with sage, lemon, garlic, scattered a little sherry over them, but still not happy. You know how difficult I am at work in the kitchen – children, wife, dogs, they all ask too many questions and want to go for a walk. I looked around – there was a red cabbage sitting on top of the onions – that's it – I wrapped each grouse in a cabbage leaf, covered the dish with foil, more foil – those silly birds always end up dry – so – in the oven, shut the door, dive into the pub down my street with shattered nerves.'

That is indeed Stephan's cooking routine and rhythm. On the way to his house for dinner, I first check the pub. If he is there, I know the worst is over and that he is ready to talk, if not take me for a walk.

Stephan continued, 'I returned twenty minutes later, refreshed, removed the cabbage leaves, left the birds in the oven another ten minutes perhaps, to brown, then a rest and the heat turned off. They were perfect. Perhaps English food must be cooked by foreigners, no?' Which is what I tried, years ago, starting with steak and kidney pie, then gaining confidence, steak and kidney pudding. Trying to forget my memories of fatty meat and watery gravy, I read different recipes and decided the dish was, after all, a daube. In went red wine, a dark stock, brandy, garlic. 'Delicious, just as it should be,' said Miles who, one October, arrived home with a white truffle. It was put to work for a week, in a bowl in the middle of six fresh eggs in their shells. Twenty-four hours later, I removed the truffle, intact, and scrambled the eggs. They were strongly permeated with that strange smell and were delicious, no need to grate the truffle over them. I took the truffle to Roxana four miles down the road. She kept it for twenty-four hours in an air-tight glass jar with six ounces of Arborio rice: risotto for herself and Tony. She brought the truffle back and I did the same. Still not exhausted, that truffle continued its shuttle service for another day or two, and finally, we were all replete.

Steak and Kidney Pie – or Pudding

Use a fairly lean piece of beef, such as blade bone steak, a cut from the foreleg that is reasonable in price and has a firm texture for long stewing. I prefer to buy a whole piece and prepare it at home. So far, no butcher will trim the meat to my liking, carefully removing fat or gristle and sinew. A piece weighing 1½lb / 750g will be reduced by a ¼lb / 100g approximately, once trimmed, and serves four. The kidneys make up the loss of weight.

1½lb / 750g BLADE BONE STEAK; 3oz / 85g BEEF SUET, or the suet around 2 lamb's kidneys; 4 lamb's KIDNEYS; 1 large ONION, finely chopped; 2 broken BAY LEAVES; a dozen crushed JUNIPER BERRIES; 1 teaspoon TOMATO PURÉE, 1 teaspoon strong Dijon or Amora MUSTARD; dash each of TABASCO and WORCESTERSHIRE SAUCE; 2 capfuls Gordon GIN; ⅓ bottle RED WINE; 2 ladlefuls of STOCK, preferably game, otherwise chicken or veal. If you don't have game stock and you do have some blue cheese such as Stilton or Roquefort, dilute a spoonful with a little liquid. It will give gaminess to the gravy without detection of the source. If making the pie, prepare PASTRY such as the one for the pissaladiere recipe (see page 43) and refrigerate shaped in a ball and wrapped. This can be done a day ahead of time, as can the stew.

The stew   Trim and cube the BEEF into 1in / 2.5cm pieces. Slice the KIDNEYS fairly thickly, about ½in / 1.25cm – my reason for this is that Tasha, not that keen on offal, can easily spot the slices and give them to Georgia and me, since we love it.

Melt the SUET slowly, in a large frying pan, preferably cast-iron. Using a slotted spoon, remove the pieces that won't render more fat after about 10 minutes over low heat. Turn the heat up to near high and fry the beef pieces in batches. Brown all surfaces, scraping and turning. Remove with the slotted spoon to a round, glass dish, about 2in / 5cm deep, 8-10in / 20-25cm across.

When all the beef has been done, cook the kidneys briefly. Remove to the pie dish. Turn the heat down again, soften the chopped ONION in what remains of the melted suet and add a little BUTTER if necessary. Stir up the scrapings and browned bits into the onions. Cook for 5 to 10 minutes.

Return the meats to the pan. Add the gin, red wine, stock and seasonings, tomato and mustard. The meat should be nearly covered with liquid. Cover, simmer 2 hours for the pie or 1½ hours for the pudding. Check towards the end for extra seasoning – stock and mustard are salty but your palate may require a pinch. The gravy should reach half way up the pieces of meat; if not, add a little wine or stock.

Turn into the pie dish and leave to cool. Roll out the pastry on a floured board. Sit the pie dish on top, draw a circle round the bottom with a blunt knife. Remove the dish and cover with the circle of pastry, moistening fingers with drops of water and pinching the edges of pastry onto the rim of the dish. Use the extra bits of pastry left to decorate the lid, with leaves, for example. Make a pea-sized hole in the middle to let out steam.

Assembled, this can be refrigerated for a day. Brush the pastry with a little egg yolk diluted with a spoon of milk and place on the lower shelf of a medium oven and bake until the pastry turns a good tobacco colour, approximately 25 minutes. (Remember to remove the dish from the refrigerator at least 2 hours before cooking, to bring it to room temperature before putting into the heated oven.)

The pudding Prepare suet pastry as for Pea Pond Pudding on page 22, using the same proportions and pudding basin. Once assembled, the pudding should not be kept waiting for its steaming for more than a short while. It will only need 2 hours to steam as the stew will have already cooked for 1½ hours.

When filling the suet-lined basin, bring the meats and gravy up to 1in / 2.5cm below the rim. So that the pudding can rise, cover the basin with foil, leaving a folded pleat across the top, then tie with string. To serve the pudding take out of its steaming pot, remove the string and foil cover, then wrap the basin in a pretty cloth and serve.

A permanent place is laid for Murray; Beaver Dam friends

Murray called, as was now the habit between us, once or twice a week. The conversation often ends without plan. But this time, I invited him to dinner, to meet Tony and Roxana who were staying for a few days. Ian was in town and would join us, then Tarfa, Patrick and Ann, both editors and mutual friends of Murray's. As it was Ian's birthday quite soon, I lay his place with a large soup tureen. Inside I put his present, a small porcelain box with a spoon of salt inside it for luck and wisdom. Roxana gave him a handsome nineteenth-century mug we had bought together that afternoon.

We had slices of raw salmon cooked in the acidity of lemon and lime juice, then olive oil, mint and parsley; a cassoulet of seafood. This took three days to prepare, much in the same way as a meat cassoulet. I used chicken and fish stock. The two, surprisingly, like each other and blend into one. I used squid, bacon, and scallops. On the evening, I transferred the dish to a large cast iron casserole and baked it for another two hours, adding, at the last minute, the scallops. By the time we ate the cassoulet the taste was strange, metallic and offensive. No one other than Roxana seemed to notice – we ate very little. The next morning, washing up, I noticed the cast iron pot was cracked with rust. This explained the odd taste. Cross, I threw it out, then changed my mind and put it in the garden to be used as a flower pot.

Murray came for supper two nights later. I gave him lentil soup, thickened with the leftovers of the veal pecorino I had given Tony and Roxana on their first night. This was much better. 'Soon,' Murray told me, 'I am bicycling my way to Cornwall with friends for Christmas. See you next year, ta-da ta-ra!' He made his goodbye noises and slipped out the door like magic.

Lamb with Pecorino
This is rich but basic. Most Italian delicatessens have pecorino, hard and soft varieties. You should use the latter, called sardo, during the cooking of the lamb. Almost chalky white, it is dry

enough to chop neatly. Sardo means Sardinian and, according to some, sardonic, which gives you an idea of its taste. The cheese is added during the last five minutes of cooking; its gamy taste permeates the dish in an earthy way.

I use a LEG OF LAMB, cut into 1½in / 3.75cm thick steaks, 1 per person. Trim the steaks of all fat and cut into 1–2in / 2.5–5cm sized pieces.

Brown the meat at high heat in OLIVE OIL until sealed on all sides. Remove and pour out the burnt fat, if any. Return the pan to the heat, add fresh olive oil, cook 1 medium ONION per person, chopped, with several finely chopped GARLIC CLOVES. As they soften, scrape up the browned bits on the bottom of the pan. The moisture from the cooking onions will deglaze the caramelising liquid. Add half a sweet RED PEPPER per person, cut in 1in / 2.5cm pieces and soften.

Return the lamb, pour over the meat and vegetables enough STOCK to come half way up. Cover and simmer on a gentle heat for 20 minutes. Add 2 or 3 POTATOES per person, cut in half or quartered, depending on their size; if new, leave on the skins. Cover and simmer for another 15 minutes. Check that the liquid has reduced to a syrupy consistency, that there is only just enough to baste the meat and vegetables. To reduce the liquid further, cook another 5 minutes, lid askew, to accelerate evaporation.

Chop into small cubes enough pecorino sardo to sprinkle over the meats and vegetables, at least 2oz / 50g per person. Cook, uncovered, barely stirring, for 2 minutes or until the cheese has just melted. There will be little patches and strings of melted cheese. Leave them, don't try to blend them in. Toss in a generous amount of chopped PARSLEY and fresh BASIL. Serve immediately.

At table pass a grater and a piece of the hard pecorino for each person to grate more cheese onto their helpings.

Afterthoughts: Toby had this the other day, it was very good even though I was stuck on the telephone and the potatoes were slightly overcooked. I tried it another time using veal instead of lamb, but that was a mistake and a waste of the veal's delicate taste. The pungency of lamb is more suitable. If you do not have stock to hand, use a combination of dry WHITE WINE, MADEIRA, a few heavy dashes of WORCESTERSHIRE SAUCE, a little water. Avoid stock cubes.

Making this for myself and Georgia another time, I forgot the RED PEPPER. I used frozen PEAS instead, since there was absolutely nothing else to hand. I put in 4oz / 100g of the peas, straight from the freezer, at the onion and garlic stage. It worked well.

End of year; dinner parties

The end of a year approached. Dinners, holiday preparations, Georgia's birthday, friends, plans and thoughts mixed and rushed along in a frenzy. I went to dinner at Tarfa's. Her apartment is full of books, up to the ceiling, and her own sculptures, dark matte metal, brutal and handsome. Her daughters were upset while watching the news of more bombing in Beirut in a street they knew and love well; I felt ashamed remembering the times I had watched similar pictures with indifference. Tarfa's food was elegant, northern, the only sign of her Middle Eastern affinity for scent appearing in a salad, lavishly perfumed with summer savory. As a hostess, Tarfa looks after her guests with eastern grace, invisibly moving the Latin and Anglo-Saxon mixture around, not letting the same pairs stick together for long.

Another dinner party. Partners on my left were talking about sightseeing in Africa. 'Once you've seen one hundred lions, you've seen one hundred lions.' I resisted barking at them, remembered Branko and felt I was the worst kind of refugee: not even an accent. I went to talk to the caterers. The food was deliciously simple. Roasted lamb, baked potatoes, salad, a varied board of cheeses, an exotic mixture of fruit in a basket. The details made the difference. The lamb was a whole sheep, roasted outside on a spit. Skin and fat were browned and crackled to perfection; bowls of an unusual hot and minty sauce were passed around the many tables. I asked the head man for the secret of the sauce. He was young, mustachioed, and happy to talk: 'One cup of sesame oil, a thick bunch of fresh coriander leaves (he made a wide circle with his big hands), three limes – skin, pith, everything – six cloves of garlic, a little olive oil, a whole jar of redcurrant jelly, dried mint (fresh too bitter when blended), a thick bunch of chives (again the same gesture, stretched to show the bunch must have been a foot long), the top part of

spring onions, two chillies or more, depending on your taste for heat.'
All this went into the blender, all at once. To keep it for two weeks, 'add
a few drops of vinegar.' The sauce was a speckled green, quite thick and
very good.

Soon, it was time to gather presents and pack a suitcase. The children
were going skiing with Miles; I was going to Geneva.

Rice for Tarfa

This is strongly scented, almost flowery. I usually serve it with a
chutney on the side, then followed with a minty, cucumber salad.
The following quantities will feed four people.

1 large ONION and 4 cloves of GARLIC, finely chopped; 1
teaspoon each of CARAWAY SEEDS, FENNEL SEEDS, COR-
IANDER SEEDS, CARDAMOM PODS, shelled; 1/2 teaspoon
each of ALLSPICE, CINNAMON; 1 1/2lb / 725g of ground
LAMB or BEEF; 1 tablespoon TOMATO PURÉE; juice of half a
LIME; several dashes of SOY; 3 tablespoons ROSEWATER;
handful whole or halved ALMONDS, skinned and lightly toasted
in HAZELNUT OIL; a handful of RAISINS (optional).

Allowing 3oz / 75g of long grain RICE per person, cook ahead
of time with a few strands of SAFFRON and TURMERIC.

Cook the onion in a large frying pan, in OLIVE OIL, stirring
for a few minutes, until almost crisp. Add the garlic, caraway,
fennel, coriander, cardamom, allspice and cinnamon. Toss and
cook a few minutes. Remove onions and spices; reserve. Brown
the ground meat in the same pan, adding more olive oil if
necessary. Turn up the heat, brown well, separating any lumps.
Keep scraping the pan as the bottom begins to brown. Return the
onion and spice mixture, stir in with the meat, lower the heat to
medium, add the tomato purée, soy, rosewater and a small glass
of water or stock. Let the liquid evaporate, the mixture stick to
the pan. As it browns, scrape up the solids. Add another glass of
water when the meat is once more almost dry. When the meat is
still just moist, a little sticky, remove from heat, add the lime.
Taste for seasoning, add SALT and freshly ground PEPPER.

Oil a ring mould, scatter the toasted almonds and raisins on
the bottom. Lay the meat mixture over the almonds and pack it
down. Fill the mould three quarters of the way up. Pack the rice

down over the meat. Lay a heat proof serving platter over the mould, turn over but leave the mould in place. Put in a medium hot oven for 15 minutes or set aside until ready to do so.

The mould will lift off easily as you serve, leaving the shaped and scented rice dish. Sprinkle the centre hole with freshly chopped PARSLEY, CORIANDER and MINT.

Christmas with Le Moustique; the table is upside down

Christmas. I arrived in Geneva Monday evening, two days before Christmas Day. I hadn't seen my cousin Miguel, my Moustique, in years. I was met at the airport: Joyce, Miguel's Brazilian wife, their five-year old son Lorenzo; Arlette, her daughters Dariane and Claudia. I brought a long and thick red winter sock for Lorenzo, filled with tissue-wrapped mysteries. Later, he sat on the floor, pensive, twisting a strand of hair into a corkscrew, examining instructions for the model of a glider; this little boy's skin was the colour of my freckles. There was Mon Moustique.

Christmas Eve. Two family friends were to arrive just before dinner, one with a freshly cooked foie gras wrapped in a cloth, the other with a smoked salmon. Joyce prepared the mantelpiece and the table, covering both in red and gold metallic cloth, candlesticks, leaves and shiny things. She gathered the cloth with needle and thread, sewed the corners so that it would fall properly. Perhaps Brazilians don't eat turkeys, but Arlette and I decided we did. We joined her and went to work. It was a little late, the butcher only had small birds left. We bought two. We couldn't find a baking dish large enough: we squeezed both onto a makeshift foil platter. Arlette made a stuffing. Sausage meat, fresh breadcrumbs – just a little – the livers of the birds, brandy, herbs, an egg, salt and pepper. She mixed it with her hands as I put more in the bowl. Onions, garlic. We smelled it. Something missing. More brandy, crumbled chestnuts, a little lemon juice, more pepper. We filled the birds, poured red wine around them and put them into a hot oven. The door wouldn't quite shut; we propped a chair against it. We each returned hurriedly at different intervals to baste the birds, check the sauce, add a little more wine, a little Madeira, a little mustard. Everyone disappeared to change, finish wrapping presents.

Almost ready, I walked past the dining-room. There were crackling noises; festive. I glanced at the table in the flickering candlelight, vaguely puzzled. The candles seemed alive and big. I almost walked on, looked again, saw little flames turn to torches. The metallic cloth had caught fire, the tree's branches touched the table and were catching. I shouted 'au feu!' on my way into the kitchen to fetch water. I heard running and what sounded like a car crashing. Back into the dining-room with a filled kettle. Miguel had turned the table over. He looked at my kettle, I looked at the debris on the floor. 'You're dreaming – we need three buckets,' he said. Seconds of laughing fright passed, the fire was out, dinner was on the floor, the table on top, its four legs up in the air, the salmon overturned but intact, and the turkeys in the oven. Some of the foie gras remained, half the china and glasses were whole. There were eight of us. The mess was gathered up quickly, ashes swept away, the table turned upright like a sailboat.

Christmas was celebrated. At midnight, we woke Lorenzo, all the windows wide open to show him the wake in the sky of le Père Noel, a custom I had forgotten. Church bells were ringing.

I returned to London on Boxing Day. I woke up on New Year's Day thinking of the upside down table; happy. I went downstairs and decided to change the finish on my kitchen table. With sandpaper, I stripped the layers of wax and an unsuccessful semi-French polish. By mid-afternoon, the surface was bare and pale. I thought of the colour of wooden spoons, after days and years of stirring sauces. Why not treat the table in the same way. Over it I emptied a bottle of extra virgin olive oil, spreading it evenly and slowly. The smell was wonderful. I left the table to absorb.

The next morning, there were shiny streaks of excess oil. I rubbed it in the table with bare hands, childishly pleased. The colour had deepened. It was going to work.

The table has remained impervious to extremes of temperature, to spills of wine or water. Scratches are part of the grain. The treatment has worked.

Index of Recipes